TRUCKS
OF THE WORLD
HIGHWAYS

TRUCKS
OF THE WORLD
HIGHWAYS

ARTHUR INGRAM AND
NIELS JANSEN, COLIN PECK, MARTIN PHIPPARD

BLANDFORD PRESS

Poole   Dorset

First published in the U.K. 1979
Copyright © 1979 Blandford Press Ltd,
Link House, West Street,
Poole, Dorset BH15 1LL
ISBN 0 7137 0994 4

British Library Cataloguing in Publication Data
21/10/82
Trucks of the world highways. – (World
 review of trucks and trucking).
1. Motor-trucks
I. Ingram, Arthur   II. Series
629.22′4   TL230

Set in 10/10½ pt V.I.P. Plantin
and printed and bound by
Fakenham Press Limited
Fakenham, Norfolk

Illustrations supplied by **Sven Bengtson** –
p.109(2); **Chrysler UK** – p.22; **Bryan Edwards** –
p.95(2); **ERF Ltd** – p.18(2); **Fiat** – p.93(3);
Foden Ltd – p.18(3); **Ford Motor Co.** –
pp.53(1), 153; **Hino Motors** – pp.2, 9, 111, 136;
Arthur Ingram – pp.13, 15, 17, 18(1), 20, 21, 57,
58(3), 69(4), 71, 72(1, 2, 4, 5), 109(4), 131,
135(2), 148, 151, 154(1, 2,), 158; **International
Harvester** – 49; **Niels Jansen** – pp.10, 31(3),
38(1), 58(1, 2), 67(2), 69(1–3), 77, 78, 79(2), 81,
84, 86, 88(1, 4), 91(1–3), 93(2), 96, 99, 100(2,
3), 102, 103, 105(1–3), 113(2, 3), 114(1), 116(1,
3), 118, 121, 123(1–3), 125(2), 129(1), 140(2),
143, back jacket; **Kenworth** – 34;
Mercedes-Benz – pp.88(2), 114(2); **Andrew
Morland** – pp.26, 29, 31(1, 2), 32(1–5), 37,
38(2, 4, 6); **OM** – 95(1); **Colin Peck** – front
jacket, pp.25, 36, 46, 51(2), 53(2), 54, 55(1, 2,
4), 67(1), 75(1, 2), 88(3), 100(1), 107, 109(1, 3),
114(3), 116(2), 129(2), 133(2, 4), 135(1); **Martin
Phippard** – pp.1, 28, 38(3, 5), 41, 43(1–3), 44,
51(1), 53(3), 79(1), 127(1–3), 144(1, 2),
147(1–3); **Saurer** – pp.7, 83, 93(1); **Scammell
Motors** – pp.113(1), 157; **Scania** – pp.62(1),
133(1, 3), 140(3), 142; **Sisu** – pp.58(4), 61;
Volvo – pp.62(2, 3), 64, 72(3), 125(1), 139,
140(1). The author would also like to thank
Willy Bos, Kees Gras, Ron Knight and Harry
Paterson for their help.

CONTENTS

INTRODUCTION

Some historians regard the Cugnot steam vehicle of 1792 as the world's first mechanically propelled vehicle for burden, for this lumbering three-wheeled tractor for cannon might well have been further improved had it put up a better performance than the 3–5 mph achieved during early trials. Others hold that the modern heavy truck has its origins in the steam road coaches of the 1820s, for without the intervention of the railways we could have enjoyed advanced steam road transport well before the end of the nineteenth century; instead it was limited to agricultural vehicles. Then there are those who feel that if we are concerned with the internal-combustion-engined vehicle we ought to look no further back than the small petrol-engined vans of the 1890s.

Strictly speaking it was the early petrol motor vehicle which spawned the modern commercial type which – with the later development of the diesel engine – has formed the basis of the world's land transport operations. (With liquid fuel reserves rapidly dwindling, of course, there are some who will point out that we have not heard the last of steam power, nor, indeed, of electricity!)

Another point worth mentioning is that when looking at some of the very early commercial trucks with their large wheels and high ground clearance we are reminded that the truck of today has yet another parent – the horse-drawn waggon or buggy. In the early years of truck history it was the horse-drawn mode of transport which was constantly referred to when questions of cost, speed and reliability were at issue.

Some years later, when the horsed vehicle had been virtually eclipsed, opposition arose between road and rail transport – a battle which still rages in some countries. But in a conflict of more recent origin it has been against the ship that road transport has pitted its claims with regard to high-value or perishable commodities. The long runs by truck from Europe to such places as the Persian Gulf and even Pakistan are now commonplace, although the route to the Far East is perhaps taking things too far, so to speak.

Throughout its long history, whether one begins in 1792, 1820, 1860 or 1890 there has been a continual battle by truck manufacturers, operators and drivers against legislation and interference of one kind or another. No one would argue with the safety laws enacted for the protection of public and employees against, for instance, cowboy-type drivers and rogue operators. Some manufacturers in fact have looked much further ahead and produced vehicles with a far better safety margin on such things as braking and cab safety than that required by legislation. What does irk the vehicle-building

Saurer tippers engaged on a Middle East harbour project.

industry is the web of complex and non-standard regulations which govern the dimensions and weights of vehicles within one country while, a few miles away, other laws apply. The best examples of this are seen in the United States where the laws even vary from state to state, some allowing the operation of 'doubles' (tractor/semi-trailer/full trailer) or even 'triples' (tractor/semi-trailer/full trailer/full trailer) over certain highways; others seemingly opposed to any high-capacity vehicle.

In some instances there are good grounds for limits on vehicle size and weight because of road conditions and bridge construction, although many would argue that heavy vehicle operators have surely paid enough taxes to successive governments to pay for routes over which optimum-size vehicles could operate safely. A case occurred in Britain in 1922 when a local authority responsible for highway maintenance and repair successfully sued a transport operator for the cost of repairs necessary to a stretch of highway which, it was alleged, had been damaged by his vehicles. This famous case – Butt *v*. Weston-super-Mare UDC – gave rise to the 'extraordinary traffic' phrase which meant that the roads were capable of handling everyday light traffic only, and anyone causing damage by the use of a heavy vehicle was creating 'extraordinary traffic' and was therefore liable for any repairs necessary.

Now this ruling could apply in two ways: either one heavy vehicle such as a traction engine could literally go right through any eggshell road surface in one go, or a contractor who had operated light horse-drawn carts along a road outside his yard might change to heavier motor lorries only to find that the road started to break up.

It was the heavy haulage specialists who probably suffered most at the hands of the local highway authorities, who reacted strongly whenever their roads gave way beneath a 60-ton load! Talk to any old-established heavy haulier and he will relate the innumerable long-distance calls from vehicle attendants asking for help when their vehicle and its load was suddenly trapped by the seemingly sound road surface giving way. Then arguments ensued about repair costs while the heavy gang with their 'jack-and-pack' technique slowly retrieved the vehicle from the ensnaring road.

Another face of legislation is that which – by means of various laws, statutes or other enactments – has limited the physical size of the carrying industry through various forms of licensing. In many European countries and America the early days of truck operation were comparatively free of restrictions so long as one paid one's way by means of taxes. But this freedom did not long continue,

for it was seen that, although the industry was expanding rapidly and there was ample healthy competition both between the trucking industry and other forms of transport and between rival truckers, it was leading to much price-cutting, which could in turn produce low wages, lack of maintenance and many bankruptcies. Some form of limitation was necessary to provide a buoyant, profitable and competitive industry but one which also provided some measure of protection for those within. The introduction of licensing naturally provoked considerable criticism all round, but those well established in the industry soon began to realize that perhaps the system had its virtues. For although limits were set on the size of vehicle fleets individually, with due regard for seasonal fluctuations and special types, it also gave protection against the wholesale infiltration by would-be new-comers. One of the difficulties of any licensing system is that of fairness and impartiality, some believing that a licence should be granted to those who prove need for a service, while others feel that the onus of proof should be on those who object.

It is probably true to say that the majority of those inside the trucking industry do not object to some form of licensing or regulation for the industry. The system that really does enrage them is that which prevails in some countries under which one transport system can prejudice the issue of licences to another. Thus we find in some parts of the world that the railways (usually state-owned) can object to, and what is more have the power of veto over, the issuing of licences to road operators. There are those who feel that this is an objectionable practice and that the most efficient system should prevail. But others take the view that if the financial resources of a country are invested in its rail system then it should be used to the full, although this rarely happens.

The modern trend is to invest huge capital sums in road networks which can be used both by commercial transport and the private sector. The cost is usually not directly funded by the road users, but is met by central government, which allocates the money that has been raised by general taxation. Whether roads should be provided by taxes paid by the road users, or by general taxation, is another bone of contention. Like so many other 'national institutions' roads are provided for everyone who cares to use them, and this is one of the arguments that has been put forward many times in the past when such issues as the 'extraordinary traffic' case mentioned earlier were argued.

In the early days of motor traffic there was a move towards funding road construction, repair and maintenance from taxes on vehicles and the

fuel used. For some reason it was decided that either the engine size or the vehicle weight should act as the yardstick in apportioning the scale of charges, which meant that one is charged for having the vehicle in the first place and then charged again according to how much it is used. Various alternatives have been mooted over the years including mileage taxes, a levy by engine power, a tax levied according to vehicle size (not weight) and the ultimate scheme of no taxes at all!

The majority of us accept that the money has to be raised somehow, although we object to unfair discrimination against certain types of vehicle on the grounds that they are considered unsightly, noisy, smelly, big, heavy or otherwise generally undesirable within our modern urban environment. There is plenty of legislation to deal with noise emission, exhaust pollution, overweight or otherwise unsafe vehicles. To levy additional taxation against one section of the road-using industry in order to subsidize another less profitable or even uneconomic one is hardly fair play.

Another aspect of anti-truck legislation is increasingly to be found in the powers granted to local authorities in certain countries under the heading of 'traffic management schemes'. These highly contentious operations are aimed at excluding wide or heavy vehicles from certain roads or areas. In some locations the boundaries of such schemes are marked by signs of the type normally used for traffic control. A recent trend is to resort to the artificial narrowing of highways by erecting obstructions to the traffic flow so as to bring the highway down to a desired width. Having effectively excluded anything wider than, say, 2 metres from passing a particular point, the local authority then has to erect padlocked gates across the carriageway in order to allow the fire brigade through! For, in official parlance, the fire engine is not a truck and so is welcome. Should this type of restriction be extended over large areas, there is perhaps a case for a series of special narrow-width vehicles which could then penetrate 'no-go' areas. Some local authorities have themselves had to purchase special slim (7 ft or 2·12 m) municipal vehicles for use in the narrow heavily trafficked streets of some old towns.

At the opposite end of the scale some local authorities have been forced into employing larger vehicles than hitherto in order to handle the ever-increasing amount of rubbish which we seem to generate nowadays, when everything comes in 'convenience' packages, immediately thrown away. Many authorities have had to look much farther afield for their rubbish disposal sites, some even resorting to the use of ISO (International

Hino have been successful in export markets, particularly with their tipper models.

Standards Organization) containers for the very long journeys. This use of containers is probably the most unusual, save perhaps for those which get stolen and used for housing in some remote parts of the world!

The container has changed the face of transport throughout the world during the last twenty years or so, for it has provided the facility for long-distance inter-continental traffic by road/rail/sea without the consignments being handled at points on the way. It has also improved the lot of the driver, for he no longer has to wrestle with heavy sheets and dirty ropes.

The vehicle itself has also undergone profound changes during the same period, for what was considered quite acceptable in the 1950s would find no place in many of the efficient fleets of today. One area in which this change has occurred probably more than any other is cab design. For very many years the truck cab was recognized purely and simply as a place of work, and the man who sat in it for perhaps 300 days a year was suitably dressed for the tasks that were an everyday part of his working life. These tasks included checking the vehicle's condition, carrying out refuelling, topping up engine oil, filling and emptying the radiator, thawing out the fuel filters, loading the vehicle by hand, sheeting up and roping down the load securely

before the driver could set off.

Once on the road this man was seated in his sparse wood-framed metal-panelled cab and was 'king of the road' indeed. If it was summer he would probably be dressed in an open-necked or even collarless shirt, with perhaps a choker scarf tied around his neck. His working trousers would probably be blue serge or grey worsted left over from an old suit and kept up by beige coloured braces or a wide leather belt – perhaps both. Boots would complete this almost regulation dress: stout black boots with laces up the front, not the fancy cowboy style so talked-of today. If it was very hot the vehicle windscreen would be open – they did open in those days – and on slow uphill climbs with the engine roaring away in a low gear our driver would perhaps be sitting towards the door in an attempt to catch any breeze.

In cold weather the opposite extremes applied. The cab was cold – bitterly cold, for heaters were 'extra', not very efficient and often in the wrong place. Most cabs were not only cold; they were draughty and uninsulated. Rags and newspapers were useful for ramming down into gaps in the floor and engine cover or for stuffing up ventilators. As the control pedals protruded through the floor there were great gaping holes which directed the biting wind straight up the unfortu-

nate driver's trouser legs. The ill-fitting sheet-metal engine cover helped leak fuel fumes into the cab, and if the engine was diesel there wasn't much heat from it either. It was usual to put an old piece of carpet or an old overcoat over the engine to stifle the noise a bit as well as providing somewhere for a nap during those interminable queues at the docks. Some drivers even took to carrying a small mattress for extra comfort when they carried a passenger or spent the night in the cab.

During the winter our driver was also suitably dressed for the weather, wearing a waistcoat, pullover, jacket, overcoat, woollen scarf, and perhaps carrying a shovel on board for the snow. A rolled up newspaper or piece of wood was generally needed too, to wedge up the window which invariably fell down every time the cab shook over an unseen pot-hole. The seats of some old cabs were also a bit primitive, with little adjustment and simply no allowances for the varying shapes of lorry drivers.

When breakdowns occurred our driver was expected to get himself out of trouble. Wheels had to be changed at the roadside, perhaps fuel lines, brake parts, road springs, half-shafts, prop-shafts as well; even sumps had to be dropped and big ends checked. All this had to be accomplished with a fixed cab, a few odd tools and a box of matches.

The modern vehicle cab is a credit to its producers, with its efficient air conditioning, more complete instrumentation, 70° tilting, plastic insulation, fully adjustable seating, clean carpeting and wall-to-wall stereo! Now our truck driver looks cleaner, less anxious and much better turned out as he glances over the completed service check sheet for his vehicle. He collects his batch of documents and expenses and places them in his briefcase. He checks the seals on the container, then climbs up into the comfortable cab. He stows his case on the bunk at the back of the cab and then decides to hang up his smart zip jacket with the company logo on the pocket. Adjusting the heater controls with one hand he selects an easy-listening cassette with the other. He goes through the pre-heat ritual before the 300 hp turbo power unit hums into life, then he checks his instrumentation to make sure the fuel tank has been filled for him, before easing the 40-ton giant into movement.

Admittedly that is exaggerating a little, but it does go some way towards showing the tremendous progress that has been made in recent years, not only in the design, safety and comfort of trucks but also the gradual acceptance that the truck driver is someone to be considered. He deserves a safe, comfortable environment in which to work; not just a little tin box stuck up front of the load.

Moroccan-assembled 5-ton Berliet with a mixed load negotiating a track in the Sahara region.

GREAT BRITAIN

Once one of the greatest exporters of trucks, Britain today
contains few independent truck builders. Everywhere there are
signs of imports from the European mainland and more recently
from the United States. As in many other countries legislation has
a restricting effect on vehicle design, resulting in
little variation between producers.

*Much of Britain's long-distance haulage has been
handled by rigid eight-wheelers in the past. In this
historic picture the Skylon for the 1951 Festival of
Britain pauses in High Wycombe* en route *for the
south bank site.*

Road transport in Britain is a very important industry, handling the major part of the freight movement within the country as well as a considerable proportion of export traffic. It has been estimated that 95 per cent of everything used is carried at least part of the way by road.

Being a temperate country there are no extremes of weather to upset road conditions, except for a very few days each year, and this probably explains why at the slightest sign of snowfall the transport system is immediately thrown into confusion. Travel to Canada or Sweden and one soon notices that the snow is an accepted part of the year, but back in Britain the gritters and snowploughs might well never turn a wheel in some winters. Luckily the summers are never hot enough to cause serious problems.

Unfortunately British transport has suffered in other ways, not least in being used as a shuttlecock between the main political parties, who seem intent on change, control, legislation and nationalization, although not necessarily in that order. Considering the upheavals that have taken place in the last sixty years – for that is about the age of British long distance haulage – the industry is still fortunate in being that indescribable mixture of state control, free enterprise, large combine, one man, licensed non-monopoly. It has been largely an industry of small enterprises and family businesses which have survived through being flexible and resourceful. With short lines of communication the small firms are able to react swiftly to changing patterns of traffic or other important issues. Very many of the drivers themselves are strong individualists and not disposed to being part of a large organization such as that which exists in manufacturing plants. A result of this is that no work stoppage of any importance occurred in the industry until early 1979. Ever since the Railway Strike of 1919 and the General Strike of 1926 road transport in Britain had shown itself to be the reliable one in times of trouble, no doubt because a large section of it was run by tough individuals who perhaps had only a handful of vehicles and were used to doing much hard graft themselves.

Even today many of the operators can trace their beginnings to the days of handcarts and horses, and they remained of a size which was easily controlled by the members of one family, who together ran the business and shared the responsibilities. Similarly, many road transport operators still carry on the same type of work as that done by their grandfathers with a pair of horses. Businesses like household removers, heavy haulage specialists, parcels carriers, timber hauliers, etc. still retain their individual character.

The aftermath of the 1914–18 war was the breeding-ground of many small businesses when a number of ex-servicemen pledged their all in acquiring one of the thousands of ex-military lorries for a few hundred pounds and set out on the highways. Some attribute this movement to a sense of individual enterprise gained while serving in the armed forces, while others argue that so many men were disillusioned by what they found when they returned home to that 'land fit for heroes' that they opted for the lonely life of an owner-driver.

Some of the individual hauliers were extremely diligent and their businesses grew out of all recognition, but others – very many others – were not so lucky and went to the wall. Whether their failure was attributable to their lack of business sense, their lack of capital, or the poor condition of the vehicles is not certain. Many of the vehicles were ex-wartime machines themselves, made available from the government vehicle dumps. Not all of them were British-built either; there were many US-built trucks supplied to the Allies during the war and subsequently returned to Britain at the end of hostilities. The Americans were quite astute in not taking them back home with them, for a whole batch of cheap ex-military equipment would have meant a depressed market for new trucks.

Not all the military trucks were brought to Britain; some remained in France and were renovated or otherwise rebuilt, and did good work for very many years. It was with the old US Liberty trucks that the French builder Willème began.

Among all the US-built FWD, Liberty, Jeffery, Pierce-Arrow, Packard, AA, USA, Traffic, Day Elder and other trucks returned from France there were a few old European machines captured from the enemy. These were duly inspected to see what could be learned and then sold off together with all

Seen loading sugar beet at a Cambridgeshire farm is this B-series ERF with SP-type cab. Operating at 31,000 kg gross it is powered by a 259 bhp Rolls-Royce engine.

the AEC, Leyland, Commer, Albion and Dennis machines which had seen active service. Naturally these trucks were in a variety of conditions, and some must have caused their new owners considerable trouble in the years to come.

Two of the names well remembered from that era are the Peerless and the Leyland RAF type. The former was assembled at the site of the government dump at Slough by using spare parts for the original US-built machines, but later introduced its own design. The latter model stood up well to the rigours of war, and its builders were so anxious to uphold their reputation that they acquired the majority of the ex-military machines and rebuilt them before putting them on sale.

It has been said that the motor truck actually grew up in the 1914–18 war because that was the first time that the military took to using vehicles extensively. They had seen limited use previously in India and South Africa. By the time World War II started the motor vehicle was the premier form of military transport.

The period between two major wars had shown tremendous progress in both trucks and road transport operations. Long-distance road services had become an everyday part of the transport scene and the vehicles themselves had progressed at an alarming rate. As usual there had been great upheavals because of legislation. There were whole reams of laws about speeds, weights, roads, bridges, carriers' licences, vehicle construction and use, lighting, road/rail co-ordination, heavy goods vehicle driving licences, trailer attendants, road signs, wage rates, hours of work, tyres and dimensions etc. Significant changes had included pneumatic tyres for the heavies, articulated trucks, diesel engines, the demise of the road steam vehicle, light-weight construction, containers, better roads, and a whole load of smaller detail changes which resulted in gradual improvements.

The immediate post-war years were to bring the biggest argument ever in the field of transport – that of national control through nationalization, brought about by an overwhelming swing to socialism by many people in the aftermath of war. The desire to control transport was nothing new, for there had been much talk of a similar scheme some twenty-five years earlier when a government report on inland transport had resulted in the grouping of the country's railways. At this time it was thought that road transport would remain merely as a feeder to the railways but, as later events were to show, they were well wide of the mark. During the ensuing period the unwieldly railways lost much of their traffic to the more efficient road services with the result that there were constant pleas for a 'square deal' by the railways, including a proposed parliamentary bill which would give the railways powers to run road vehicles where required. This last piece of legislation was vigorously opposed by the road lobby and luckily it never reached the statute book.

But to return to 1947, we find that the Transport Act passed by parliament created the British Transport Commission, which set up the Road Haulage Executive to acquire, either by voluntary or compulsory purchase, those parts of the road transport network which were engaged primarily on long-distance work – meaning over 40 miles – during 1946. So in 1948 began the process of acquiring the major part of private road transport operations but excluding certain types of traffic – among them bulk liquids, explosives or inflammable goods in special vehicles, felled timber on special vehicles, household furniture removals, meat and livestock haulage and the carriage of abnormal and indivisible loads in special vehicles. Local carriers were limited to operation within a 25-mile radius of base unless permits were obtained from the Road Haulage Executive for specified traffics and journeys.

Within five years the second, most important bill was before parliament. This time it was a move away from restrictions and resulted in the passing of the Transport Act of 1953 which created the Road Haulage Disposal Board, set up with the intent to sell off a large part of the nationalized road haulage fleet. So the pendulum swung away from the plain red lorries and green vans of British Road Services to a much more lively scene of operators and individual liveries. Since that time, as the country has veered to the Left or Right, there have been rumblings about further controls should the political climate reach certain extremes. So far this has not transpired, and free enterprise and controlled road transport share the market.

As the pattern of trade and traffic has changed, so road transport has had to keep in step. Not so long ago almost everything was moved around in small lots which entailed constant handling of

individual items or small cases or bags. The introduction of pallets and fork trucks has gone a long
way in improving cargo handling, and the more
recent idea of shrink-wrapping has helped prevent
losses even further. The ISO container has been
the one single item which has helped more than any
other in creating a smooth flow, although the first
cost is high and some seem to suffer through rough
handling. The use of demountable bodies is
another step towards reducing terminal delays and
increasing the flexibility of the vehicle. Any system
which enables the motive unit to be used inten-
sively is worth study by operators anxious to
reduce the unit cost of every load moved.

One drawback of the highly sophisticated
equipment now the order of the day is of course its
cost, and many of the transport operations are now
being handled by larger organizations which have
the large financial resources required. This in turn
has led to another gradual change, that of labour,
for whereas many of the transport units are small
with perhaps only one or a handful of vehicles,
there has been a recent tendency for the larger units
to become the focal points for organized labour.

*For carrying overlength loads the use of a small
'dolly' trailer is popular in Britain. Here a pair of
AEC 'Mammoth Major' eight-wheelers operated by
Highland Haulage cross a bridge in Glasgow.*

This state of affairs became public knowledge very
early in 1979 when the first large-scale official
strike of lorry drivers took place with devastating
results, though only a particular sector of the road
transport industry was involved. One good thing
that came out of the strike was that people forgot,
for a while at least, about all those dreadful 'jug-
gernauts', and there was a pause in all the anti-lorry
propaganda while they bemoaned the fact that food
supplies were in peril. Nonetheless, anyone who
has the slightest connection with road transport
will be fully aware that it is an industry that survives on being flexible, and that hardly a day passes
without the appearance of some new problem.

A study of trucking operations in Britain in
comparison with those in many of the larger
countries of the world reveals that the average
British trucker is better off than he makes out.

Though now an active member of the EEC (European Economic Community), Britain is still an island, and retains much of its own identity in the matter of trucking operations. Of course many EEC rigs visit Britain every day, and maybe just as many British rigs ply European highways with cargoes for international destinations, but while Britain is slowly hounded into accepting more and more EEC legislation it is still very much its own master when it comes to internal trucking.

In considering the current system of licensing and truck legislation let us start with the truck driver. Although a driving licence for an automobile can be held at the age of seventeen in Britain, the would-be trucker normally has to reach the age of twenty-one before legally being able to get behind the wheel of any truck over 3.5 metric tonnes unladen weight. 'Normally', because the government was recently forced to relax this rule in the face of high unemployment and union pressure. Obviously the intending trucker has to pass a truck driving test to prove his competence, and there are many private truck driving schools all over Britain that take the novice trucker out in a rig and get him up to the required standard; the current average cost of such tuition is around £200 ($380). An employee of a large company may be more fortunate, for many operate their own truck driving school or area school formed with other companies in the vicinity – in which case tuition could be free of charge. The employee in question would probably have to sign a document committing himself to pay for a certain proportion of this tuition should he leave the company within a twelve-month period.

Before he can take to the road with the school rig the learner trucker has to undergo a medical examination and hold a provisional HGV (heavy goods vehicle) licence. When the driver is thought to have reached the required standard he will be tested, for around two hours, by a government-appointed driving examiner, and on passing this test he will then get his full HGV licence. These licences are issued in addition to the normal automobile licence and are graded according to the type of rig or truck in which the driving test was taken. Class 3 covers two-axle rigid straight trucks; class 2 covers three- and four-axle straight trucks; and class 1, the most highly prized, covers tractor semi-trailer rigs of any size and gross weight. A

1

2

3

1. Sutton and Sons of St Helens, Lancashire were the operators of this twin-steer six-wheeler and drawbar trailer on long-distance haulage.

2. 1978 saw the introduction of the ERF M-series 16-ton gross chassis, with either Gardner or Dorman engine.

3. A 265 bhp Rolls-Royce engine powers this Foden 'Fleetmaster' articulated outfit which features a Motor Panels cab and is rated at 38 tonnes gross.

class 1 driver can drive vehicles in the lower grades 2 and 3, but not vice versa. With the coming of automatic gearboxes in trucks anybody taking a driving test with a truck fitted with such a transmission would get a licence with an 'A' suffix, for example 1A, 2A or 3A, and cannot then drive a truck fitted with a manual gearbox. However, drivers of regular gearboxes may handle automatic-transmission trucks.

The licensing system for truck operation is the same for large multi-national carriers as it is for small owner-operators, a fair deal which cannot be said to exist in every country of the world. Provided that a trucker has business, can prove his truck or trucks will be kept in safe mechanical condition, and that no other licensed truck operator objects, then the new trucker is in business and gets his operator's licence, known as the O licence. This operator's licence is issued by the government-appointed Licensing Authority, and in general the licence is permission to operate a specified number of trucks, tractors and trailers on the public highway, carrying any load anywhere; it is as simple as that.

A garbage haulier can truck steel and a dump truck can haul furniture quite legally, that is of course providing they could find such obscure loads in the first place. The one O licence covers a whole fleet of vehicles and trailers, and will stipulate the exact number, with perhaps a margin for expansion to cover predicted future fleet enlargement, although this margin will be quickly removed if the fleet is not actually enlarged within the time limit specified by the Licensing Authority. The Licensing Authority (LA) lays down hard and fast rules that any O licence operator must stick to, and wields judicial authority, with the power to revoke the licence and to impose some large fines on offending operators.

The first obstacle the new truck operator has to surmount is that of getting a commitment from a shipper or manufacturer that he will actually give that trucker hauls, and this has to be put in writing in the form of a letter of intent from the company concerned. When submitting this letter of intent to the LA the hopeful operator leaves himself open to objections from already licensed truck operators in the area, and it is up to the LA to decide whether there is a real need for this newcomer. It may well be that the shipper who is backing the new operator

has already used all the operators in his area and obtained poor service from them. The LA, though government-controlled, has a duty to the trucking industry in general in that it has to limit the number of trucks in use on British highways to an efficient and economic number, thus ensuring that those vehicles actually licensed are utilized to the full; this helps to keep their owners in business, and that is the name of the game!

All applicants for O licences have to prove beyond doubt that vehicles thus licensed will be maintained to the legal standard currently in force in Britain. For an owner-operator or small fleet the normal method is to make a contract with a local commercial vehicle workshop to carry out routine servicing or repairs, and a copy of this contract has to be furnished to the LA for approval. If the applicant is a large fleet operator then he will obviously want his own workshop facilities; however it is no use a company planning to operate maybe a hundred trucks building just one service bay, as the licensing authority will have to inspect plans and servicing facilities before any O licence will be granted. Vehicle maintenance plays a large part in the British truck licensing system, with the LA not only sending out inspectors to make surprise visits to operators' premises to inspect both vehicles and servicing equipment, but also instigating roadside checks of trucks; any faults found could result in the truck operator losing his O licence.

The whole operator's licence system as it stands today came into being back in 1971, replacing a complicated system which had three main groups of truck licences. These licences not only stipulated the distance from base within which the truck owner must operate but also the types of commodities allowed to be carried.

Once licensed, the operator faces other problems. Before he can legally turn a wheel both the truck and its load must be insured, and the truck must have excise tax paid on it. Excise tax is calculated on the unladen weight of a truck, with trailer if hauled, and can run into many hundreds of pounds each and every year. There are four main categories for maximum permitted gross weights of highway trucks in Britain: two-axle rigid straight trucks can gross 16 tons, three-axle rigids can gross 24 tons and four-axle rigids 30 tons gross weight. The maximum permitted gross for any vehicle and combination of trailers is 32 tons, and this applies whether the rig is an articulated tractor/semi-trailer rig or a truck and full trailer drawbar combination. The articulated rig can measure up to 15 m (a fraction over 49 ft) in length, whereas the drawbar rig can be some 18 m (59 ft).

A well-designed truck and trailer drawbar rig can accommodate two 24 ft bodies, one on the truck and one on the trailer, giving a total floor length of 48 ft, which still allows some 11 ft for the vehicle cab and drawbar coupling to stay within the 18 m maximum length limit. However the 15 m tractor semi-trailer rig can just haul a 40 ft semi-trailer within the legal length limit, and the tractor has to have a carefully sited fifth-wheel coupling to accommodate a sleeper cab and not be overlength.

While the maximum gross weight is low compared with the 38- and 40-tonne limits found in Europe and the 36 tons in America, the British axle weights are far higher than those allowed in the United States. With a 6.5-ton single-tyred axle, and a 10-ton dual-tyred axle there is no legal need for the three-axle tractors which are popular in America, although an extra axle may be needed eventually when the British government (it is hoped) raises permitted gross weights from 32 to 38, 40 or even 42 tonnes. Since 1970, when Britain first talked about joining the EEC, both truck manufacturers and vehicle operators have been looking for such an increase in permitted vehicle gross weight. Europe has a fairly universal gross weight of 38 metric tonnes, although Belgium

Originally designed for the British Road Services operating companies, the Scammell Crusader 4 × 2 tractor was later available to all comers. A larger six-wheel version was popular with heavy hauliers.

allows 40, Italy 44 and Holland a massive 50 tonnes, with countries such as France and Spain allowing the use of the heavy-weight 13-tonne axle. (1 tonne = 0·984 tons.)

To avoid the embarrassment of having no models appropriate to the proposed new gross weights, British truck manufacturers embarked on a crash programme of model development in the early 1970s – although nobody could predict with any certainty just what increase, if any, would be made. Initially, increases up to 44 tons gross were spoken of, at which weight a three-axle tractor would become a necessity; many such prototypes were produced and shown at truck exhibitions in Britain. The basic concept behind increased gross weights for Britain is to make operations easier when trucks travel to and from the continent of Europe, where higher gross weights are allowed. ISO containers 40 ft in length, for instance, could easily handle 25-ton payloads, but because of the 20-ton limit in Britain many overweight containers arriving from overseas would need to be partly unloaded before they were allowed to travel over British highways. When Britain originally joined the EEC the government were more interested in increasing gross weights than they are today; however they were very much against any increase in axle weights, stating that the British 10-ton limit was the maximum which British roads were engineered and constructed to bear. When the EEC transport ministers' meeting at the Brussels headquarters suggested an 11-tonne compromise axle weight for all countries the French put up fiery resistance to the proposal, retorting that they had been using the 13-tonne axle for many years, and that their whole truck industry was built around the use of such axles, including the spending of many hundreds of thousands of francs on a new axle plant at the state-owned Berliet truck plant.

Today the position has changed little, except that most maximum-weight British-built vehicles are designed and constructed for anything between 34 to 38 tonnes, so as to be able to take advantage of any increase in vehicle gross weights as and when they are introduced.

As one might expect truck speed limits differ from those applied to other vehicles. There is an out-of-town limit of 40 mph generally on ordinary single- and dual-carriageway roads, with a 60 mph limit on motorways. In order to keep trucks in

Foden S83-cabbed 10 ft 3 in. wheelbase tractor with Cummins NHC250 and Foden eight-speed gearbox, coupled to three-compartment liquefied petroleum gas tank semi.

what disparaging politicians think their proper place, they are banned from the third and fastest lane on motorways, and so often have to bunch up in the slower two lanes – stuck behind some slow-moving car driver who refuses to pull over and wrongly assumes, no doubt, that the trucks could easily pull out and overtake him in the third lane.

A particular feature of the British truck scene is that it is split into two very different spheres of operation. For any new or existing truck operator, whether running a large or small fleet, there is a choice between purely internal, round-Britain trucking, or going international and taking on hauls across Europe; maybe to Greece, Turkey, the Middle East or even farther – to Africa and Asia, for example.

Most existing companies got off the ground trucking on Britain's highways, and then expanded to cover international routes. However, because of the difference in gross weights and operating conditions found in Britain and the rest of Europe, different types of trucks are usually specified for each type of operation. A truck operator choosing to operate within the bounds of Britain will usually select equipment to meet British legislation, and a typical 32 tonner would be a two-axle, non-sleeper cab tractor with around a 220–250 bhp (brake horsepower) diesel engine and an eight- to ten-speed gearbox, but would probably have a design gross weight of 34 to 36 tons as a step towards any up-grade in vehicle gross weights.

Obviously it is impossible to make generalizations, as vehicle choice depends on a wide variety of circumstances. However, there is a distinct swing towards higher-powered diesels, even for purely internal trucking, with around 250 bhp being the norm. With many companies operating higher-specification trucks on international hauling, the experience gained from using such machines will often reflect on the vehicles used on British highways, which explains why many heavy-weight tractors with sleeper cabs and a high gross weight specification, usually including a diesel of around 290 bhp, are now on the roads.

British highways and toll-free motorways get pretty crowded, and trucks jostle each other for position in the lines of trundling vehicles that seem to congest most inter-city routes. Five hundred miles is considered a long haul in Britain, with 200–250 miles being closer to the daily average and the majority of trucks engaged on local and short-haul work often hauling ISO containers and ships' cargoes to inland destinations from the many ports situated around Britain's coast.

Britain has a fair percentage of owner-operators and small fleets. Really large fleets are rare, and a fifty-vehicle fleet would be considered a large operation. The largest single fleet of trucks belongs to the state-owned British Road Services (BRS) group, which is now split into seven area operational companies. BRS was formed back in 1947 just after World War II, when the Labour government of the day decided to nationalize the important forms of transport in Britain and so took control both of the nation's railway companies and all the long-distance road haulage companies to form the latter into one huge combined trucking fleet.

Today the BRS empire is much smaller and is split into seven regional operating companies with each group having its own vehicle colour-scheme. BRS operations include short and long haul, parcels, contract, tankers and even truck rental. Since 1968 BRS has been part of the state-owned National Freight Corporation (NFC), a holding company for all state-owned road transport undertakings, including Pickfords, the nation's largest heavy hauling firm and also household removal company, and National Carriers, which was formed from the British Rail Sundries Division and took over the railway road vehicle fleet. National Carriers handles local railfreight deliveries and also operates specialized parcels services, such as for the fashion and pottery industries. Freightliner Ltd was owned 51 per cent by the NFC until January 1979, when it was returned to the ownership of the British Railways Board. Freightliner handles container traffic by rail and road. It is an interesting and expanding company which specializes in full loads inside containers which are sent by rail between the Freightliner terminals in Britain, and a next-day delivery is usually guaranteed. Trucks are used for the termi-

Largest vehicle marketed by Chrysler in Britain is the 300-series RP38 which offers models grossing up to 38,000 kg. The vehicle originates from the Chrysler España plant.

nal handling (either Freightliner or of the haulier or producer) and ideally for this traffic system the point of loading/unloading should be convenient to the container depot, for the whole concept is undermined if a long road haul is necessary.

When Britain entered the EEC it opened the gates for an invasion of European-built trucks to be sold in Britain alongside British vehicles – on equal terms. Gone were the old import tax and trade barriers, and in that section of the market comprising trucks of over 28 tons gross weight there are now around twenty-five different makes of truck battling for an annual market of around 10,000–14,000 vehicles. A market leader in this gross weight category might be selling 3,000 trucks per year, while at the bottom of the scale another might only sell 100. A British company selling just 100 trucks a year might have problems staying in business, but a European manufacturer exporting trucks to many countries can do good business with just 100 sold in each of several markets.

Britain has surprisingly few home manufacturers in the 32 tonner segment of the market. Bedford, ERF, Foden, Leyland, Seddon Atkinson and Scammell build vehicles within the United Kingdom, while Chrysler import vehicles from their Spanish plant, and Ford build their Trans-continentals in Holland. Surprisingly enough it is the small independent companies who sell the most trucks in the face of stiff opposition from European rivals; companies such as ERF, Foden and Seddon Atkinson (owned by International Harvester) all fight it out at the top of the sales chart, which must reflect their workmanship and reliability.

British trucks also offer a form of custom-engineering, similar to US-built trucks. While virtually all trucks built on the mainland continent of Europe are constructed solely from parts manufactured at their own plants, British trucks can usually be specified with a choice of Gardner, Rolls-Royce or Cummins diesels, and a wide variety of gearboxes and axles. Seddon Atkinson build their own axles; Foden build both axles and gearboxes and, of course, the British Leyland empire build every component themselves including the engines. Over the years Leyland rationalization plans have meant a sad cut-back in the number of model ranges within the British Leyland empire, and we have seen the demise of such long-standing makes as Albion, AEC and Guy, which leaves just the Scammell and Leyland names to carry on.

Bedford, the British overseas operation of General Motors, recently went into production with heavy-weight trucks and tractors (having built only light- and medium-weight vehicles since their start in 1931). The Bedford TM range offers trucks up to 42 tonnes gross vehicle weight and was the first to install Detroit Diesel engines in any great quantity for the general trucking market. The 32 tonner which features the narrow D-series cab has a Detroit Diesel 6V71 series engine as standard, while the heavier 38 tonner has the H-series wide cab and has the 8V71 series Detroit Diesel installed as standard. The Detroit Diesel is a thoroughly tried and tested unit, with over one million in service around the world, but it is only just gaining acceptance in Britain, and 1978 saw the introduction of the Cummins Formula E290 engine to the TM range.

Ford offer the Transcontinental range in Britain; it is built with parts from several Ford plants in Europe plus a cab from Berliet. It is finding customers right across Europe as well as Britain, although strangely enough it is one of the first trucks to get Cummins engines *en masse* to the continent of Europe.

ERF, which stands for Edwin Richard Foden, is an independent yet thriving truck producer based at Sandbach, Cheshire. The firm produces a range of trucks between 16 and 38 tons gross weight, the popular B-series models featuring Gardner, Cummins or Rolls-Royce diesels, fitted with a steel-framed, glass-fibre-panelled tilt cab. The recently introduced M series – without doubt the highest quality 16 tonner on the British truck market – is built with a projected working life of ten years, and although fitted with a 188 bhp Gardner aluminium 6LXB diesel engine, it is the first vehicle to offer the British trucking industry the option of a Dorman engine.

Just down the road from ERF at Sandbach is the works of Foden, another independent truck manufacturer. This firm is in no way connected with ERF as the Foden brothers split up to form two totally different companies a long time back. Foden are probably best known for their robust eight-wheelers which are highly acclaimed among tipper operators, and of course Foden build a range of off-highway dump trucks as well. Foden must surely rank as the company which has changed its cab designs more often than any other. It is not at all unusual for Foden to have at least three different cabs available at any one time, usually with glass-fibre and steel options. At one time Foden even built their own diesel engines, of two-stroke design, and in the 1950s and early 1960s an approaching Foden truck could be identified easily by the screaming of the Foden two-stroke engine.

The Seddon Atkinson combine was formed when Seddon took over Atkinson Vehicles, and the newly formed alliance was then itself taken over a short time later by the American International Harvester Company. IHC had tried unsuccessfully in the mid-1960s to launch conventional Perkins-powered Loadstar trucks and tractors into the UK truck market, but the takeover of Seddon Atkinson has turned out very well, and today the company are the top-selling British heavy-weight truck manufacturers. Three distinct model series are produced at the Oldham plant, the 400 series 38-ton tractors offering the usual Gardner, Rolls-Royce or Cummins diesels, while less-powerful engines from the same stable are offered in the four-axle rigid 30 tonners. The 300 series is a three-axle straight truck aimed primarily at ready-mixed concrete and dump truck operators, and a special feature is the use of the IHC DT–466 diesel. The lighter 200 series two-axle is for operation at 16 tons gross and features the IHC DT–358 engine producing 134 bhp.

NORTH AMERICA

Looked upon by many as the originators of the world's most
attractive trucks, the North American continent epitomizes the
free-enterprise Western way of thinking. This is highlighted by
the large, powerful and glamorous trucks which daily ply the
long and sometimes lonely stretches of trans-continental
highways.

Kenworth cabover double-heads down the highway
alongside the Columbia River which separates
Oregon from Washington state.

THE UNITED STATES

There is an infectious sense of urgency running through the American trucking industry. Whether it is Christmas Day or Good Friday, mid-day or midnight, summer or winter, trucks move on. Cab doors bear slogans – 'Pulling for the Nation' or 'Don't track it, truck it' – evidence that the American trucker knows the value of his job and wants others to appreciate it too.

America is a big country, with some states at opposite ends separated by distances of thousands of miles. But a first-class highway system joins together even the most far-flung places, and where there's a highway, you'll always find a truck.

In New York city, not only Autocars and Macks from the factories nearby will be seen, but also chrome-adorned Peterbilts and Kenworths from the western regions, their drivers bleary-eyed after the long haul just completed, the load of fresh produce unspoiled. At any truck stop, from Arizona to Washington, lean Texans in cowboy boots and stetsons are on view, hauling cattle to the meat packing plants. Things have changed a bit since the 55 mph limit was introduced; at one time these Texan truckers were considered the fastest in the land. In fact the passing lane in the United States is always referred to as the Montfort Lane, a tribute to those truckers from Montfort Truck Line who at one time had their rigs geared to speeds of 100 mph or more and who hustled their loads from west to east in record time, rarely leaving the fast lane.

But despite its great size and super road network, trucking in the US is not always the glamorous job it's cracked up to be. Some of the trucks used by the owner-operators would 'blow the mind' of a trucker in Britain or France, the chrome and paintwork alone representing a small fortune. But with each state having its own ideas on how the trucking industry should be run, trigger-happy police on the look-out for trouble and the vastly differing weather conditions faced by most truckers, life is often anything but easy.

There's little doubt that individual state regulations constitute the biggest hazard faced by

This Mack conventional with bottom dump semi of the Gobble Trucking Company is pictured at one of the famous truckstops with easily visible sign.

1

truckers hauling over long distances. Not only are trucks required to have a licence plate (purchased at the going rate) if they are to haul in any state other than their own, but drivers must comply with the peculiarities of that jurisdiction concerning gross and axle weights, driving hours, etc. Violators of these rulings, whether deliberate or accidental, can expect quick and costly action from the police or weigh-scale personnel.

Some state authorities are positively anti-trucking. One of the best known is Pennsylvania, a state which has persecuted truckers ever since the days trucks first started taking business from the railroad. It is not uncommon to see as many as five or six patrol cars lined up over the brow of a hill, each just waiting to catch speeding offenders. When speeders are caught, they are pulled over as a group, the police waving cars and trucks on to the hard shoulder. This obviously helps to keep the state coffers filled, but recently CB (Citizen's Band) radio has helped to keep the income from Pennsylvanian radar traps down a little, warning truckers of traps ahead. 'Fuzzbusters' and other anti-radar systems are illegal in Pennsylvania, as in

1. Not all Peterbilts are chrome-adorned beauties; some are just plain-Jane workhorses like this heavy tractor which hauls twin tank trailers.

2. Interior of the Little Gypsy Peterbilt pictured on page 32. No room for muddy boots in the luxurious interiors offered by the more discerning manufacturers.

many other states, and truckers caught with them in the cab, even if the device is disconnected, face stiff fines and confiscation of the unit.

The weather, too, plays havoc with the American trucker. He might leave California in mid-winter *en route* for New York or Chicago; during the journey he could encounter everything from dust-storms and typhoons in the mid-west to temperatures 40 degrees below zero in the northern and eastern regions. Such conditions play dirty tricks on equipment and until the advent of multi-viscosity oils many a 'southern' trucker with heavy, summer-weight oil in his sump and summer diesel in his fuel tank found himself stranded with a rig

2

that refused to start again should he have to shut it off in a northern town. But even the advances made with components and lubricants cannot always overcome the worst conditions, and only experience – much of it learned the hard way – can teach a driver from Louisiana how to control his rig in the icy treachery of a Wisconsin winter.

The trucks used by American truckers are as varied and individually styled as the truckers themselves. Of course, there is a geographic preference which often prevails. For example, truckers in and around Illinois will be more inclined to buy and operate a Hendrickson than truckers in New York, while New York operators will be far more likely to favour a Mack from nearby Allentown or possibly a White Road Boss or Road Commander from Cleveland in Ohio. Until recently Brockway vehicles were popular too on the eastern seaboard, but the closure of the plant in Cortland during 1977 saw the end of the line for this rugged marque.

Out west, Peterbilt, Freightliner and Kenworth trucks dominate the scene, many being equipped with cosmetic options such as chrome wheels and exhaust stacks, air conditioners and fancy paintwork. Even fleet trucks benefit from this pride in appearance – which seems all-important in states such as California and Oregon. Ford, GMC and International trucks may be found almost anywhere, these being available through an extensive dealer network which spans the country. Models of smaller manufacturers, such as the CCC, Oshkosh, FWD, Marmon and others, are generally confined to the area in which they are built, distribution networks being limited.

Specifications vary considerably too, under the influence of legislation, use and owner preference. Western rigs may feature air ride suspension and light-weight aluminium components, while in Michigan (where weights of up to 153,000 lbs gross are permitted) the emphasis is on heavy-duty items, big power and over-sized tyres. Trucks running in more than one state are very carefully specified, and are designed to comply with the laws in several parts of the country. Special equipment on these rigs may include sliding fifth wheels, air-lift axles on trailers and sliding bogies, all of these devices helping truckers to stay within overall

length limits or to meet inner axle spread requirements, kingpin to rear of trailer measurements and
the host of other regulations seemingly designed to
drive truckers into an early grave.

There are many differences between American
rigs and those produced by other countries of the
world, differences which relate to size, weight,
configuration and so forth. But one of the biggest,
though least obvious, differences concerns the
actual choice of options open to the US buyer
compared to his European or British counterpart.

A salesman in Britain, for example, when putting together the specifications for the vehicle he is
hoping to sell, will have a very limited number of
options open to him and his customer. He may
have the choice of three or perhaps four diesel
engines in a certain chassis, say a 32-ton gcw (gross
combination weight) tractor unit, an equally
limited number of transmission options and probably only one drive axle, though this might be
offered with two different final drive ratios. Apart
from this the only other choices will concern
wheelbase (though usually only one is offered),
power steering, tyre equipment, spare wheel and
carrier, and an illuminated headboard! Similarly
limited numbers of options apply to most weight
categories, and though a 16-ton gvw (gross vehicle
weight) rigid may be offered in three wheelbases,
the engine/transmission combinations offered are
usually even more limited than those for the 32
tonners.

In the United States the story is completely
different. A data book used by a Mack truck salesman can be a huge volume weighing up to 15 lbs,
and the list of options is almost endless. American
truck buyers usually have at least half a dozen
choices on every component from the front suspension to the rear cross-member, and salesmen have
to be familiar with each and every component and
its suitability for different applications. Items that
are carefully selected by most fleet buyers may
include batteries, starters, fuel tanks – aluminium
or steel, square or cylindrical, with steps or without
and with choice of capacity – driver's seating, air
cleaners and fifth wheels. And, of course, all
buyers specify engine, clutch, drive axle(s) and
front and rear suspensions.

The American system naturally means that fleet
operators have, or can have, very fine control over
what components are specified and installed in

1

2

1. This Diamond T looks rather sombre in its plain black and white colour scheme. Despite popular belief the majority of trucks are not resplendent in fancy paint jobs.

2. A sleeper-cabbed GMC cabover pictured at a truckstop. Note array of CB antennae and useful vizor, though the paint job is a subdued scheme.

3. Typical 'Michigan Train' is this Detroit Diesel-powered GMC 9500.

1

3

4

2   5

1. *Mack conventional tractors appear to be more popular with bulk hauliers and dump operators than the more normal over-the-road carriers. This one hauls aggregates.*

2. *Attractive but not too flashy best sums up the paint job applied to this Peterbilt conventional 'Little Gypsy', which also sports a fair array of aluminium and chrome fittings, air horns and additional lights.*

3. *Seen at a truckstop are two of the most popular cabovers for long-distance hauling: White Freightliner and Kenworth.*

4. *Even the travelling Holy Ghost Evangelist Revival chooses a box semi to bring its message home to the masses.*

5. *Peterbilt conventional with a reefer load of perishables. 'Petes' are a very popular truck with owner-operators.*

their trucks, regardless of the chassis selected. Indeed, some of the largest US fleets, and most government departments, put out tenders to truck manufacturers that spell out exactly what components are required right down to the grade of bolt to hold the alternator bracket in place and the heat to be maintained in the cab at waist level if the ambient temperature drops to 40 degrees below zero. In addition these tenders will stipulate the maximum tare weights of vehicles in road-ready condition, and woe betide the salesman delivering a truck overweight. Buyers have been known to refuse delivery of vehicles deviating as little as 200 lbs from the quoted weight, and on government orders – where big-volume hauls are often the case – the results to the unfortunate manufacturer can be disastrous.

Initial cost is sometimes not such an important factor as operating or running costs, and being able to select components and monitor their cost-effectiveness is a science in many large American fleets. Some companies, particularly the lease fleets, can determine to three decimal places what each individual component costs in terms of maintenance and eventual replacement, and these data are effectively used.

Record-keeping is recognized as being a vital ingredient in any successful operation, but while computerized records are kept by the big fleet operators, the owner-operators at the opposite end of the spectrum often have little idea of their costs. And if costs are not known, then it is next to impossible to estimate compensatory rates. In this respect the owner-operator is at a great disadvantage, having neither the time nor the expertise in most cases to calculate exact cost figures and profit margins. Couple this to the fact that fleet operators buy everything from their trucks to their diesel as much as 20 per cent cheaper than the owner-operators by virtue of their bulk-buying capacity and one begins to wonder how the owner-operator remains in business at all.

The answer would seem to lie in the fact that the owner-operator, while ostensibly an inadequate businessman and record-keeper, can and does provide a better service than fleet operators who are usually bound up in the complexities of trade unionism and federal regulations. The service provided is, if you like, more personal, and to shippers service is frequently more important than cost.

There is still much controversy, at both fleet and owner-operator level, regarding the relative merits of the cabover and the conventional type of vehicle.

Cabovers obviously have an advantage where overall length limits are kept to 55 ft – a figure that still exists in some states – but maintenance records show that cabovers are about half a cent per mile more expensive to operate than conventionals.

Although the claim that cabovers provide a far rougher ride than conventionals no longer holds true in most cases, an argument still frequently heard on behalf of the long-nosed bonneted conventionals is that these offer far greater resistance to injury in an accident. While such an argument might well sound ill-founded to European truckers, 90 per cent of whom drive cabovers, the point does have some validity in the United States, where the incidence of head-on collisions involving owner-operators is fairly high, the reason being, one supposes, because owner-operators drive long hours at high speeds and sometimes fall asleep at the wheel. Whatever the reason, sales for cabovers and conventionals in the United States in recent years have been about evenly split, with most cabovers entering service with fleet operators, and owner-operators buying up the conventionals.

That is not to say, of course, that *all* the cabovers are purchased by fleet buyers. It is a fact that manufacturers such as Kenworth, Peterbilt and Freightliner will build special long sleepers married to the cabover cabs which are eminently suitable for husband and wife teams or for owner-operators who spend extremely long periods of time on the road. These sleepers incorporate such features as air conditioning, radio speakers, reading lights, wardrobes and even television. The top of the line versions such as the Airodyne, marketed by Kenworth, even feature washbasin and toilet.

There are literally dozens of sleeper units offered in the United States, ranging from the narrow, claustrophobic types fitted to the conventionals to the integral, double-berth variety more often installed on cabovers. However, there are some 60 in. deep units on conventionals, but these are only practicable where overall length limits do not pose a problem.

Entry to sleepers mounted on conventionals is via a narrow crawl-through aperture which is usually the same size as the rear window of the cab which it replaces. The crawl-through space is fitted

'Fantastic', was the photographer's word for this Kenworth K-100 tractor with eight-axled semi-trailer used for hauling coiled steel in Michigan.

with a rubber 'boot' which flexes when the cab moves on the frame. These sleepers are usually strictly 'one-man' affairs and the most common width accepts a 36 in. wide bunk, although they range from only 24 in. to about 40 in.

A fairly recent development is the 'walk-in' sleeper for conventionals, a type which, as its name suggests, allows the driver to walk in (albeit in a crouched position) rather than negotiate the narrow and awkward crawl-through aperture. These walk-in types are usually factory installed, unlike the add-on sleepers which are usually mounted by sleeper box specialists and which come in steel, fibreglass or aluminium.

The sleeping compartment on cabovers is necessarily rather less claustrophobic than those on conventionals, but is still a far cry from the European style of sleeper, having no windows, a more private entrance arrangement afforded by small walls at each end and considerably more interior padding and appointments. Their use is different too inasmuch as sleepers on US trucks are frequently used by teams of drivers, one of whom sleeps or rests while the other drives. It is for this reason that

heavy vinyl curtains separate the sleeper compartment from the cab, thus reducing noise.

Still another type of sleeper found on some American tractors is a strange construction known as a dromedary box. This may be used as either a sleeper-cum-living quarters on long haul rigs, such as furniture hauliers, which can stay away from home base for months at a time, or simply as another freight-hauling box. Dromedary boxes are obviously only found on tractors with an extra-long wheelbase which can accommodate them between the rear of the cab and the front of the trailer, and they are almost always installed on cabover tractors for reasons of overall length.

Many myths are perpetrated about US truck stops, the amount of money a trucker earns and his working conditions. In most cases, particularly off the main arteries of the United States, truck stops are little more than small town cafés which cater to truckers as well as to tourists. Some truck stops, admittedly, are vast oases, with facilities ranging from full service for rigs to sleeping accommodation, showers, and shops for the driver. But these stops, found at some major intersections on cross-

1. Setting up a dust cloud is this Cummins-powered International Transtar heading down a dirt road in Washington.

2. A Mack cabover tandem with box semi moves off the weighscale while the queue behind waits patiently.

country highways, number far less than the rather more humble types found on the secondary highways across the nation.

Truckers can and do earn big money in some cases; but onlookers should not be fooled into believing that the operator of the lavishly decorated wide-nosed Peterbilt is rich and the company driver, in his plain vanilla job, poor. As is the case in most countries, there is a high percentage of failure among owner-operators and only a few survive long enough to be able to buy eventually (and pay off) that chrome-plated, 450 hp conventional they dream of.

On the other hand, some company drivers are remarkably well paid, and have the benefits of someone paying out holiday pay, unemployment insurance premiums, sickness benefits and pension schemes. Unfortunately, however, the company driver is frequently faced with lay-off periods, and the high wages earned for, say, nine months of the year are, when taken over twelve months, only average. Drivers employed by construction companies, driving ready-mix trucks, gravel dumps or timber trucks are among those hardest hit although periods of lay-off frequently extend to include other industries too. However, those drivers employed year-round, who are prepared to haul over routes that can easily amount to 2,500 miles per week (three round trips from Chicago to Saint Paul, for example, is not uncommon) can earn wages that are double the average income for the nation.

In recent years the trucker has been called the modern folk hero of America, or the present-day cowboy. The rig he drives, whether hauling asbestos or zinc, perfume or poison, beer or bricks has been designed specifically for the task it performs, and the man behind the wheel is almost an integral part of it. While still alive, still vibrantly active, the industry has also become a legend.

1

2

3   4

1. *Quite rare by American standards is this Kenworth drawbar combination: most operators prefer straight trucks or semi-trailer rigs.*

2. *With a choice of over 650 models, 20 diesel and 10 gasoline engine options, the Ford Louisville line of conventionals is popular in both the medium- and heavy-weight sections of the market.*

3. *Surely one of the last Diamond T trucks produced was this beautiful example.*

4. *Kenworth conventional with raised-roof 'Transorient'-style sleeper.*

5. *Ford's big cabover, the CL-9000, introduced in 1977, seen here at the Ford proving ground. It is one of the most advanced highway tractors available in the States today.*

6. *The fury of the pickets was unleashed on these two Autocar dumps in a spell of strike breaking during the 1978 coal strike.*

5

6

CANADA

Canada, the northern neighbour of the United States but with only a tenth of its population, was for many years regarded as having an inefficient and out-dated trucking industry. Today, however, the rôles are reversed, and truck operators in many of the United States look enviously northwards to the country which permits higher gross weights and higher speeds than almost any US state. Certainly some shortcomings may be found in the legislation covering the movement of freight by truck in Canada – and one of the most obvious is the absence of uniform weight laws across the huge country in which the flow of goods is mainly from east to west and back.

This lack of uniformity means, in simple terms, that a truck operator running equipment from, say, Ontario in the east to the western seaboard province of British Columbia is obliged to specify and buy tractor trailers which can comply with the gross weight rulings and axle spacing legislation for each of the other three provinces traversed *en route*. Inevitably the result is that there is some sacrifice in payload, and while this may not seem terribly serious, it does mean that the vehicle is not running at peak efficiency in terms of productivity. And competition is such in Canada that productivity can never be ignored.

There are several reasons why uniform weight laws are desirable and one of the most obvious and important is the competitive threat from the ever-present railway system.

One has only to watch the smooth operations at Montreal's super-automated 'hump' or marshalling yard to realize how quickly a 100-car freight train grossing in the region of 8,000 tons can be put together. And even the most dedicated trucking supporter cannot deny the logic in the railway's claim that one loaded freight train staffed by a team of engineers and brakemen probably totalling less than six or eight people is more efficient in terms of fuel and manpower than one hundred or more tractor trailers, especially when the distance to be travelled is 3,000 miles, which is not uncommon.

Yet, despite this indisputable advantage offered by the rail system, the growth of the trucking industry has continued to outpace its rival, and this may be explained in one word, *service*. For in Canada, as in the United States and other countries, the might of the railroad has not been able to overcome the enthusiasm of the trucking industry in spite of biased government intervention in areas, such as legislation and finance, which have always favoured the rail.

Where trucks score most heavily, of course, is that they are able to travel to areas off the beaten track, areas which in many cases have been abandoned by the railways because they were thought unprofitable. This ability to provide a regular and dependable service to communities which would otherwise have no life-line has doubtless contributed significantly to the continued expansion of trucking, though it stands to reason that operators would far sooner run their vehicles between major industrial centres with full loads than service several small and widely spread-out towns with LTL (less than truck load) traffic.

Here, provincial government legislation has helped balance the scales a little, and quite often operators having licences to transport freight between two major centres will also have a licence requiring them to serve an area which is far less financially rewarding. The terms of the licence are such that no matter how little freight has to be moved, the carrier is required to make that run, and while this may seem grossly inefficient it is the only way in which to guarantee that small outlying districts in remote northern areas of Canada will receive their supplies.

Regulations governing licences to haul freight, stipulating gross weights, lengths, heights, driving licences, mechanical fitness, power-to-weight ratios and twin or triple trailers are dealt with by provincial governments, and the federal government intervenes only in areas such as the maximum number of driving hours.

This system, as mentioned, leads to some areas of dispute between neighbouring provinces, especially on the question of weight laws. Ontario, for example, allows combinations grossing 140,000 lbs, while its western neighbour Manitoba allows only 110,000 lbs. In British Columbia, tractor-trailer combinations may stretch out to 72 ft (21·8 m approx.) while in Ontario the law was recently amended to allow an increase from 65 ft to 68 ft 10 in. (19·7 to 20·9 m approx.). Alberta is the only province which currently allows triple trailers, confined to specified highways.

However, the system is not nearly as complicated as that which exists in the United States, where each of the contiguous forty-eight states has

Ford's most popular line, after almost ten years on the market, is still the conventional Louisville. This owner-operator example is jazzed up a little by the chrome bumper and grille surround, fancy paintwork, sleeper box, CB and stereo aerials.

its own laws, many of which seem almost deliberately designed to be incompatible with those of neighbouring jurisdictions. Canada has ten provinces and two territories which means, on numbers alone, that the problems are four or five times less acute than those of the United States.

Along with the effects of legislation, Canada's harsh climate and widely varying geographical conditions play their part in determining how a vehicle should be specified. British Columbia in the west is mountainous yet not too cold in some parts during winter, while Saskatchewan and Manitoba are quite flat and horrendously cold. Ontario, because of its huge size (412,000 square miles – more than four times that of the United Kingdom) has widely varying conditions, and the eastern seaboard provinces suffer from poor roads and the ravages of air-borne sea salt.

Because Ontario is both the most prosperous and most densely populated province it is not surprising that several of the truck manufacturers have assembly plants there. Mack, Crane Carrier Canada, International, Ford and GMC all produce some trucks in Ontario although in the case of the last two companies the majority of the heavies are still imported from the United States. Quebec has the Montreal-based Kenworth assembly plant and Nova Scotia the Scot truck factory. Scot is one of the two 100 per cent Canadian-built heavy truck

firms in business today, the enterprise being owned and operated by the K. C. Irving group of companies which owns most of the business in the province of New Brunswick.

In the west British Columbia is host to White's Western Star and Freightliner Canada division (in Canada at present Freightliner and White are still not divorced) and to Pacific, the other Canadian manufacturer. A range of two-axle rigids or straight trucks is also assembled in Coquitlam, British Columbia, by Hino, the Japanese manufacturer which has been making a determined attempt to penetrate the Canadian light truck market for the past three or four years. In 1976 Peterbilt rather belatedly entered the Canadian trucking scene, and they too have their assembly plant in British Columbia.

In recent years some interesting examples of Canadian heavy vehicles have come and gone. Of these, probably the best-known was the Hayes, a heavy, specialized vehicle designed specifically for logging operations in Canada's vast woodland areas. The Hayes was first introduced in the 1920s but disappeared from the scene in 1975 after unsuccessful takeovers by Mack and, later, Kenworth. During its existence the company was a low-volume producer, but nevertheless extremely interesting examples of the marque were sold to heavy haulage companies in countries such as Spain, which does not produce a line of really heavy-duty vehicles.

The Sicard was built in Montreal and was conceived originally as a 'special purpose' vehicle such as a snow plough or street sweeper. However, in 1937, about ten years after its inception, the Sicard range of vehicles broadened out to include regular highway vehicles and dump trucks. A fairly wide range of vehicles, including highway tractors, was offered until 1971, at which time the company ceased operations. The Kenworth plant in Montreal is now located on the old Sicard factory site, and the company was for a short period before its closure taken over by the Paccar group.

Two much more recent entries to the market were the Edmonton Alberta-built Universal Carrier and the Rubber Railway Company truck which was built for a short time in Cambridge, Ontario. Less than fifty examples of each of these vehicles were built, although each offered certain advantages which could not be obtained from other manufacturers at the time of their introduction.

The Universal Carrier represented a deviation from normal North American practice in that it utilized a twin-steer, tandem-drive concept popularly known in Britain as an 'eight-wheeler'. The vehicle was designed primarily for use in the ready-mix concrete industry and was very utilitarian in appearance, employing a half-cab design. But it did offer operators the advantages of stability and high payload, the latter being increased still further by the addition of a fifth tag axle which was located at the extreme end of the chassis frame. Gross weight of the vehicle was given as 85,000 lbs, which meant that about 13 cubic yards of concrete could be carried in the mixer drum – but although the vehicle enjoyed some success, competition from the larger manufacturers saw its demise only a year or two after its introduction in the early 1970s.

A similar story can be told of the Rubber Railway Company (RRC) truck which emerged in 1973. This unusual truck employed a novel articulated frame method of steering and 8×6 drive – features which offered both reduced turning circle and greatly improved traction. In addition to these already desirable features the RRC offered operators axle spacings of 72 in. on the New Chalmers hollow rubber spring suspension, enabling them to take full advantage of provincial weight laws. RRC trucks were sold in limited numbers to most of the major ready-mix fleets in Ontario, and before its demise operators from 2,000 miles away in Saskatchewan and Alberta were investigating its potential. It disappeared from the truck-building scene mainly, it was learned, because of financial difficulties, though it seems likely that these would have been overcome had the vehicle continued to sell at its initial rate.

About ten examples of the Peninsula vehicle were built around 1960. These big cabover tractors with their set-back front axles were frequently referred to as 'boiler platers' by the drivers because the cab was constructed of heavy-gauge steel similar to that used in shipbuilding! Needless to say the cabs never wore out, but lack of expertise in construction resulted in axles running out of line, engine and transmission failure through mismatching, and other faults. It is believed that all the vehicles sold went to owner-operators who could not obtain the necessary finance for other

1

2

1. The Chevrolet Bison is the 'sister ship' to the GMC General and has similar appearance and options. In the colours of Glengarry Transport, this rig has many extras, including sleeper box.

2. Hauling dressed lumber from northern Canada is a highly competitive business, so companies go to great lengths to ensure maximum payloads.

3. Immaculate GMC 9500 conventional with ridge pole type tilt semi-trailer. This particular model has recently been replaced by the Brigadier.

trucks. Apparently Peninsula were prepared to pin their future on the risky business of owner-operators making a good living, and evidently it was a gamble that didn't pay off.

When one considers Canada's widely varying climate of arctic winters and almost tropical summers it becomes easier to understand why so few imported vehicles have found their way into the country. After all, where else in the world do drivers need air conditioners, auxiliary heaters and winter fronts on the same truck? Still, a few optimistic manufacturers have tried to peddle their products in this demanding area – and almost without exception they have failed miserably. In most cases the failure to sell was brought about by an unwillingness on the part of the manufacturer to modify vehicles for Canadian operations, or by an inability to provide after-sales service – never an easy task in a country as huge as Canada. Among those who tried with mediocre success were Commer and Leyland, the latter company even having an assembly plant in Longueil, Quebec in the 1950s. Others who never really got off the ground included Foden, Scammell, Fiat, MAN,

Not the most popular model, though this was no reflection on its reliability, was the B-73 Mack conventional, which offered a wider range of engine and driveline components than the rather better-known B-61 model.

Nissan, Mercedes and even Tatra from Czecho-slovakia.

There was failure too with engines, most of which were of British origin. A 180 hp Rolls-Royce diesel installed in several chassis including Autocar, Hayes and White, proved to be horribly unsatisfactory, as did the Perkins line of automotive diesels. The Gardner and Leyland diesels met with rather more success, although these too were far from ideally suited to the cold winters. The Leyland 600 and 680 engine were installed in the Canada diesel, a truck which was built by the Can-Car division of Hawker Siddeley in Canada during the mid-1950s and which employed a mixture of Leyland and North American components. While not many of these were built, several are still in use in 1978 in Saskatchewan, where they are employed on road construction projects by a paving and asphalt company.

Since the energy crisis of 1973–74 most of the larger trucking companies in Canada have been focusing their attention on energy conservation, or 'fuel efficiency' as it has become widely known.

The Cummins Engine Company reports that about 70 per cent of all the diesels sold by them are now 'Formula' engines, which offer improved fuel consumption through reduced engine speed and better brake specific fuel consumption characteristics. In addition to the fuel-saving engines offered by the manufacturers add-on devices such as clutch fans, which operate for less than 5 per cent of total engine operating time, are proving to be genuine fuel savers, as are cab and trailer-mounted aerodynamic devices. Radial tyres are also becoming popular, and a trend towards lower geared speeds in the region of 55 mph to 65 mph is also apparent.

In some cases fuel savings of as much as 25 per cent have been achieved by companies seriously concerned with cutting their fuel costs. In some applications it is considered that automatic transmissions will reduce fuel burning still further, and Allison is now claiming that its range of truck transmissions can meet or better any manual-shift transmission on the market in terms of fuel economy.

Surprisingly, while giant strides have been taken at the heavy end of the scale, very little has been accomplished with light- and medium-weight trucks, most of which still use gas (petrol) for fuel. International with its 466 diesel, and Cat with its 3208, are enjoying some success in this area, as is the Japanese manufacturer Hino which offers a complete vehicle. But the vast majority of local delivery vehicles are still 'gassers' (petrol-powered) and there is not really a diesel engine available for installation in chassis with designed gross weights of less than 24,000 lbs.

GMC recently introduced a diesel for their light-weight half-ton pick-up range of vehicles, but the price premium of almost 25 per cent on the price of the truck is hardly likely to encourage operators to make a switch to diesel, especially when it is remembered that diesel is more expensive at the fuel pumps.

In order to draw attention to this problem area some provincial governments have already instructed their transport authorities to investigate the need for light- and medium-weight diesels. It appears likely that once this need is confirmed – which is almost certain – then pressure will be brought to bear upon manufacturers to produce diesels, and on operators to use them. There has also been some talk about the possibility of eliminating vehicle engine 'idling', a practice which is widespread in Canada, probably due to the climate. There are, after all, very valid reasons for not wanting to shut down a diesel for short periods of time at 30 degrees below zero. The same is true of private cars, which also undergo restarting problems at very high outside temperatures. However, while it is generally accepted that by stopping idling a great deal of fuel could be saved, there seems to be some doubt as to whether such a law could be effectively enforced.

This, then, is trucking in Canada, an industry which although similar to that of the United States in appearance has some very big differences in practice.

True, the equipment is often of American origin, but the alert observer will notice a wide variety of axle spacings and suspension systems not found in the United States, as well as considerably more vehicle configurations. Most states have laws which still favour the five-axle tractor-trailer and, as a result, this is the rig most frequently seen in the United States. But in Canada manufacturers have been able to produce vehicles which take full advantage of provincial weight laws and which differ radically from those of America. The Columbia-built dromedary 'B' train is one splendid example of this.

Another major difference between the neighbouring countries concerns regulations, and it is probably fair to say that while Canada's vehicles equal those of its southern neighbour, its laws don't. As a result trucking is less regulated and truckers enjoy more freedom. Hours of work are seldom enforced, weigh scales are easily by-passed and speed zones are frequently ignored. In these cases the regulations are there, but they are not enforced. (This is not so in the United States where 'Smokey' in many states views the trucker as easy prey.) In a country the size of Canada, it is just as well that this 'pioneer spirit' is allowed to live on. In terms of overall productivity, few countries can match the record of Canada's trucking industry.

AUSTRALIA

The pioneer country of the Southern Hemisphere, Australia
boasts plenty of interesting trucks, although the vast majority
are imports. From the bustling coast zone to the lonely interior
desert, this continent contains the world's most spectacular
truck trains.

*This Kenworth rig was photographed in the eerie
light of a total eclipse of the sun; only the street light
is white!*

Once called the 'Land of Opportunity', Australia is roughly the size of North America and yet is still vastly underpopulated. It has a large central, semi-desert region – the 'bush' or 'outback' – which supports virtually no human life at all. Most large cities and towns are sited around Australia's extensive coastline, the well-populated cities usually being at least 500 miles or so from the next similar community. Without doubt the most densely populated regions are those of Queensland and New South Wales states, in the south-eastern corner of the continent.

Australia is a land of striking climatic contrasts, for while some areas suffer bone-chilling cold waves, others – such as the semi-arid outback areas – record temperatures as high as 55°C (151°F) in the shade! Tropical Queensland is deluged with an average of 350 in. of rain each year, yet other regions are limited to an annual rainfall of just 8 in. at best.

The Australian trucking industry is just as varied. Trucking conditions in Australia today are physically tough, and a distinct breed of both truck and driver has evolved over the years to cope with local conditions. Operating conditions and trucking laws are, however, frequently rather mediaeval. A lot of current trucking legislation actually dates back to 1933. Then, because of the primitive highway conditions, no one thought of restricting driving hours, and this freedom exists today; however, the recently established National Association of Australian State Road Authorities, otherwise known as the NAASRA, is working towards some major changes in Australian trucking legislation – above all a greater uniformity of laws from state to state.

NAASRA recently introduced a blanket gross weight figure of 36 metric tonnes for normal highway trucks, which converts almost exactly to the American 80,000 lbs figure, for both semi-trailer rigs and draw-bar combinations, and it is planned to increase this figure to 38 tonnes within three years. Another piece of legislation copied from the United States was the introduction of weight laws based on the American bridge weight formula which allows for 5.4-tonne single-tyred axles, an 8.5-tonne dual-tyred axle and bogie weights which vary from 15 to 16.5 tonnes depending on the state concerned. The introduction of the American-based bridge weight formula gave American origi-

nated trucks, with their set-forward front axles, a distinct advantage over typical European trucks, and this has led not only to a high popularity for American vehicles but also to many European and Australian truck manufacturers producing trucks with front axles set well forward and thus manufacturing vehicles which are unique to Australia.

The country groans under overloaded trucks, and a massive 41,000 trucks were booked for overweight offences in 1977. As the state weight inspectors get tougher with offenders and increase fines it is expected that more notice will be taken of the legal weight limits. While each state has few fixed roadside weighing stations there are also many mobile teams of weight inspectors who can set up their equipment virtually anywhere and on any highway, hoping to catch the unsuspecting trucker with their portable weighing equipment.

While the largest railroad systems are orecarrying freight lines situated in Western Australia, it is the Eastern railroads which are giving the trucking industry a hard time. With little regard for economic sense the railroads are even undercutting their own fixed contract rates to freight forwarders in an all-out effort to get more traffic. This practice is detrimental to their own profitability, for while the major Australian freight companies estimate they are already sending some 60–75 per cent of their freight traffic by rail, the railroads are still losing a vast mountain of money. In the well-populated state of New South Wales the railroads are supposedly losing a massive one million Australian dollars every day, and they did actually lose a record $274 million during the last financial year, so the loss-making railroads are not only helping to put many truckers out of business; they are generally keeping freight rates at an uneconomic level for all concerned.

Another nasty piece of Australian legislation concerns the Road Maintenance Tax which every trucker has to pay, supposedly for the upkeep of public highways, and this can easily run into many thousands of dollars each year. RMT inspectors seem to have powers of arrest, search and access almost anywhere once an unfortunate trucker gets into arrears, and such people are often hounded like criminals. An even nastier law is the one which states very clearly that should a trucking company fail to pay RMT or attributed fines, then its owners or directors can be held personally liable, so a budding young executive could be given a director-ship one day and lose his house the next.

Life can seem pretty tough for the Australian trucker, but if he happens to be an owner-operator things get even grimmer. Owner-operators represent a large majority of the truck drivers in Australia today, and there is one law which really hits them hard: a law which dictates that by virtue of being an owner-operator the trucker shall be classified as a businessman. This may not sound much in itself, but very basically it alienates the trucker/businessman from consumer protection laws designed to cushion the private citizen. This means that when the repair shop does a faulty job that leaves the trucker stranded miles from any-where, or when that new spare part falls apart after just one trip, or even when a very straightforward guarantee job goes sour and the truck dealer tells the trucker to get lost, then the owner-operator is in real trouble. As an ordinary citizen he would be entitled to advice and legal help from the consumer rights council, but by being a dreaded owner-operator, thus a businessman, the council will give him no help: he is expected to hire and pay for his own lawyer as would any other businessman. By classifying the small-time one-man-one-truck owner-operator in the same league as large corporations there is no way that the owner-operator can expect to win unless he has a watertight case and plenty of dollars in the bank. So when the repair shop puts the wrong part in an oil pump and the

engine seizes up in the outback, who can the owner-operator turn to if the shop refuses to help?

While Australia is seemingly riddled with some of the meanest trucking legislation around, it has, however, attracted some of the best trucking equipment from around the world. To safeguard jobs for Australian workers the vehicle import tax system discriminates heavily against those trucks imported in a fully assembled condition, and in order to be competitive, or even saleable, trucks are therefore shipped into Australia either in parts or completely basic kits. Many manufacturers have tried and failed to get established on the Australian truck market, and those that have failed have not necessarily had bad trucks to offer but have not managed to grasp the basic Australian trucking requirement. The really successful companies have been those that include anything from 50 to 80 per cent of parts from Australian manufacturer sources, thus enabling the resulting trucks to be truly custom-engineered to meet not only Australian trucking legislation but also the exact needs and requirements of the Australian trucker. While most of the top manufacturers from all over the world are represented in Australia today, the vehicles being built there often bear little resemblance to their namesakes in the far homeland.

In the 1950s and early 1960s the Australian heavy-weight truck scene was dominated by Leyland and International Harvester trucks, with German-built Mercedes Benz medium-weight trucks also very popular. Today it is the American-originated heavies which dominate the big rig scene, a change which had strange begin-nings in a quiet revolution in 1962. At this time D. & E. Cameron, a trucking company hauling strawberries and brussels sprouts from Sydney to Melbourne – a distance of 600 miles – imported five Kenworths direct from the American manufac-turer in Seattle and used them over this route. These S-model conventional KWs had a short hood, narrow sleeper cabs and were fitted with a 6V71 series Detroit Diesel. Because the previously operated vehicles had not performed too well the Kenworths were an instant success. Other truck operators observed their outstanding overall performance and also ordered S models direct from Seattle. From these very small beginnings a powerful legend grew which was to lead to Ken-worth setting up a company in Australia; and even

The ACCO range of Internationals are manufactured in Australia. This example is a 2150B model and was registered in Victoria.

today most Australian truckers sincerely believe
that any vehicle that comes from America is the
height of perfection!

Peterbilt, the sister company to Kenworth
within the North American Paccar group followed
KW to Australia but was curiously unsuccessful,
and this marque was eventually withdrawn from
sale. Diamond Reo met the same fate. White,
Autocar, Ford and Mack, however, are all selling
in large numbers with vehicles which are built
specifically to meet tough Australian operational
conditions. Because of the popularity of glass fibre
cabs in Australia, Mack uses them for its F-model
cabovers, employing an Australian company to
mould them to the original lines and contours of
the F-model metal cab. An interesting footnote to
this is that an Australian-originated truck manufacturer called Leader also buys the same Mack-
style cab from the glass fibre moulding company
and installs them on its own Leader trucks, so they
bear obvious resemblance to Mack products.

Leader, a company with interests in the
Australian trucking industry for more than forty
years, established its truck manufacturing plant at
Toowoomba, Queensland in 1972 with the aim of
achieving the greatest possible Australian content
in a truck. Initially light- and medium-weight
vehicles were produced, but more recently
heavy-weight trucks and tractors have been introduced, all of which are powered by Caterpillar
diesels. The other Australian-originated company,
RFW, also build heavy-weight trucks and tractors
but specialize in all-wheel-drive purpose-built
vehicles and even buses and fire trucks.

One of the few British-originated companies to
stay in the big league over the years has been
Atkinson. Taken over long ago by Seddon to form
Seddon Atkinson, then again acquired by International Harvester, the long-standing name of
Atkinson still survives in Australia on a truck
which is Australian from the ground up. The big
Atki is designed to take on the best that America
can offer: it even looks like a big American cabover
and features spider spoke-type wheels and various
engine options including Gardner, Cummins or
Detroit Diesel and, of course, a glass-fibre cab.

Leyland group vehicles are still to be found in
Australia and such once-famous names as Guy and
AEC have faded into history as the all-embracing
Leyland badge has taken over. In recent years the

1

1. *This beautifully preserved Diamond T logging tractor is seen fully loaded and parked alongside a more recent Volvo N-series outfit on a dirt forest road. Logging is a hard life for trucks, and older models such as this soon face replacement.*

2. *Pictured with a pair of typically Australian livestock trailers is an example of the imported Deutz with its rather unusual but well tried and tested air-cooled diesel.*

Leyland Marathon and the Detroit Diesel-powered Scammell Crusader (renamed Leyland, of course) have been introduced on the market to combat the waves of American-originated vehicles, although the latter seem to have too big a share of the market to be dislodged now. The small Leyland Terrier is available with a de-rated version of the Rover V8 petrol engine, and other interesting vehicles include some unusual Bedford KMs fitted with Detroit Diesels and often with a second steering axle to form 'eight-wheelers'.

Many European trucks are also to be found in

2

Australia including Fiat from Italy, Mercedes and MAN from West Germany and both Volvo and Scania from Sweden, and most of these manufacturers build 'eight-wheelers' specifically to meet local operating requirements. Scania had certain difficulties when they entered the Australia truck market as they initially sold right-hand-drive vehicles similar to those built for the British market, and these were heavily penalized, as were most other British and European trucks, because of their set-back front axles. The tandem-drive Scanias were also too heavy because their double frames and heavy bogies resulted in as much as a 1.5 ton payload reduction compared with the average Kenworth, White or Atkinson.

Scania decided that the chassis needed for line-haul highway operation in Australia would need to be as close as possible in looks and axle spacing to the United States-derived vehicles, this being what the Australian market required. So Scania in Australia used single-frame rails on the tandem-drive models and set the front axle forward by over 500 mm, and fitted spider spoke-type wheels to reduce weight even further. This new series became known as the LK and is typical of the type of custom-engineering and research that is needed to produce a top-selling truck in Australia today.

Because of Australia's relative proximity to Japan it is only natural that every make of Japanese truck is currently available in Australia, and Hino, Nissan, Fuso and Isuzu have managed to carve for themselves quite a sizeable chunk of the truck market. However, whereas Hino and Nissan prefer to market their products under their own badge name both Isuzu and Fuso have marketing agreements with established Australian truck manufacturers. Isuzu are marketed by General Motors and are in fact sold in Australia under the Bedford name, Bedford of course being the GM British truck manufacturer and already established in Australia. Chrysler Australia sells Mitsubishi Fuso trucks under the Dodge-Fuso badge and so, like Isuzu, these Japanese trucks have the benefit of a large, widely established sales and service back-up.

Contrasts in size and load capacity are most striking in Australia today with pint-size tiny Honda micro-vans making delivery rounds in the city suburbs and monstrous 'outback' road-trains hauling combinations of trailers up to 150 ft in length and weighing perhaps 130 tons. The Eastern state of New South Wales does not allow the operation of road-trains, but outside the NSW area trucks are bigger and longer, adding on trailers to form lengthy combinations which operate on a permit-only basis. A semi-tractor can haul two trailers but a rigid straight truck can haul three full trailers, so often a train of about 150 ft in length is formed.

Length regulations tend to be somewhat elastic in the sparsely populated sectors of the Northern Territory, such as Western Queensland and the northern half of Western Australia. In these areas the police cannot possibly patrol the hundreds of miles of remote roads and for this reason some road-train operators hold the view that no one is guilty until caught. It goes without saying that over-length trains are not paraded in front of the local police station!

To obtain permission to operate an Australian road-train on public highways the operator has to send an application form to the Commissioner of Police for that area. Apart from indicating such items as route, number of trailers and types of commodities the applicant also has to provide a highly detailed report about his rig. This report must include such information as axle loads and spacings, engine bhp and torque rating, number of gears, and even the size and ply of the rig's tyres. The written application form, which is returned to the operator when authorized, must be kept with the rig at all times and must be produced on demand of the highway police.

There are many common-sense reasons why such monstrous rigs are to be found on Australia's outback roads today. First there is the sheer size of the country. (The approximate size of Australia's land mass equals the whole of North America plus Alaska.) The railroads operate in general only around the coastline, and planes are just not up to the task of hauling big cargoes at economical rates, so freight has to move across the interior regions by road – and it makes good sense to move as much as possible at one time.

Unfortunately, as the road-trains get bigger and heavier farther into the outback so the state of the highways gets worse: a full tarmac two-lane highway usually leads into a two-lane dirt road with a central tarmac 'weather' strip running down the centre. In theory when two vehicles approach each other, and each is in the centre of the highway, they should both pull over a little and pass each other on

1

2

3

1. *Shipped from Britain in ckd form and assembled at the Ford plant near Melbourne, the D-series is suitable for the 28-ton gross sector of the market.*

2. *An example of the imported MAN range is this 9.230 model with widespread tandem semi-trailer.*

3. *Carried on 15 axles and grossing in the region of 100 tons, this Mobil Oil tank road train carries bulk supplies from terminal to town depots.*

the left; however, in practice, once a road-train gets rolling the driver is hardly likely to want to pull over for a mere car, so the car driver will have to try to get right off the road as a hundred tons of thundering, dust-billowing rig goes roaring past!

Once into the really remote outback areas and central Australian bush regions all signs of civilized highways disappear, and dirt roads more akin to farm tracks are the only link between distant communities. Dusty, riddled with pot-holes and ruinous to suspension in the hot and dry season, these tracks become washed-out bogs in the wet season, and it is all too easy for a rig to get bogged down to its axles so that nothing short of a D8 bulldozer can rescue it from being stuck for maybe three months until the roads dry out again. Australia must be one of the few countries that builds roads through rivers instead of bridging them, and in the wet season, when the friendly ambling stream or ford becomes a raging torrent, the driver will have to get out of his cab frequently and wade ahead to feel where the road is – and of course every time the rig stops there is a greater risk of it getting stuck.

Recently Northern Queensland was devastated by the worst flooding of the century, and all over the state roads were flooded and washed out leaving many trucks stranded. Caught in the middle of this particular flood were no less than sixteen 36-tonners hauling refrigerated trailers belonging to the Frigmobile company. Some drivers managed to drive their rigs through the rising flood waters to the nearest township but others were not so lucky. The refrigeration equipment on the trailers was powered either by gas cylinders or electricity, and some drivers were lucky enough to be able to plug into the mains at the nearest town, but many of the stranded trailers had to have fresh gas cylinders delivered by boat. One enterprising driver obtained permission to sell off the entire contents of his trailer to local townspeople who were running short of supplies. When the floods finally subsided some of the trucks were still marooned as the flood waters had so badly affected the roads in Queensland that pot-holes up to 20 ft deep were left, and some of the rigs were stuck for a further three months waiting for road repairs.

Obviously most trucks make their hauls in the dry season, when temperatures outside can often reach 50°C. and the rig has to travel across barren countryside without sight of other vehicles for days

1

on end. In conditions like these the outback trucker becomes something of an adventurer, but an accident or illness in such remote territory could prove fatal. Once the outback roads dry out they are lined with deep ruts which can put the most rugged truck suspension to the test, and many drivers would think twice about taking a four-wheel-drive Land-Rover over such roads, let alone a multi-trailer rig with over 100 tons up! For many years trucks and tractors with twin-steering front axles were regarded as a must for negotiating the pot-holes and ruts found on the outback roads, as the extra axle gave added stability over such terrain; however in recent years the type of vehicle used for road-train operation has changed. First, modern power-steering enables the driver to retain control of his truck even with just a single steering axle, and a change in Australian truck legislation allowing a semi-tractor to haul two complete trailers has meant a swing away from rigid truck and trailer combinations to semi-trailer rigs.

One of the most common hazards found along the outback highways is the kangaroo (known in Australia as the 'roo') and these animals present a real threat to the trucker at night when they often jump into the path of approaching trucks. A large bull kangaroo can demolish a glass-fibre cab in a collision. For this reason outback trucks are fitted with a heavy steel 'roo-bar': a crash-barrier device used to provide frontal collision protection for truck cabs and to nudge cattle from the path of the truck as well. In tilt cabs the roo-bar is constructed with removable pins which allow it to swing down out of the way, although more than one driver has been known to test the strength of his glass-fibre cab by hydraulically tilting it against the still firmly fixed steel roo-bar . . . with predictable results!

While many Australian trucks are air-conditioned, there are times when the trucker is better off without it, and some outback drivers prefer to use only a large fan fitted to the inside of the windscreen pillar. For if a driver had to step from his cool, air-conditioned cab into maybe 50°C. of searing heat to change a wheel, the exertion of the task in such intense heat could easily make him pass out – and this could easily prove fatal in areas of total desolation where days could pass before another vehicle came along.

2

3

4

1. Atkinson tandem cabover with Australian cab.
Note tri-axle semi is carried on dual tyres.

2. Fancy seeing this coming down your local High
Street! A massive Foden-powered road train of a
few years back with the old British-style rigid
eight-wheeler from the days when there were strong
links with the mother-country.

3. Although they were never really popular, some
operators used the 'platypus' trailer idea which
enabled them to haul bulk liquids one way and deck
cargo on the return. A good theory, but heavy and
expensive in practice. Example shown here is hauled
by an F-series Volvo tractor.

4. Driving road trains in the outback is difficult by
day and often dangerous by night. This Mack tractor
has a powerful marine searchlight mounted in the
centre of the 'roo-bar' to light the way.

WESTERN EUROPE

Contained within the patch-work of the old Western European countries are the busiest truck routes of the world. While the majority of trucks are from the older established European factories, variety comes through the increasing numbers of trucks originating in other areas.

French road haulage personified: Camions Bernard
with tilt semi-trailer outside the roadside café.

NORWAY, FINLAND AND DENMARK

Road transport is the only means of communication and commerce in many countries, and this is particularly true in northern Norway, Sweden and Finland. Above the Polar Circle railways are very limited, and shipping lines are of little importance, except for the forwarding of bulk freight – in which case trucks are necessary to take the shipped-in goods farther afield.

In Norway distances are great and roads often extremely narrow, twisting and mountainous. They are often unsurfaced gravel or tar-sprayed earth tracks, and numerous small wooden bridges still exist. Really big trucks are obviously out of the question, except around southern coastal areas where there are a few miles of divided highway. Here the maximum axle load is 10 tonnes, or 16 tonnes for a bogie arrangement, while on country roads up north loads are restricted to 8 and 12 tonnes respectively. However, many Norwegian operators have maximum 38 tonne gcw combinations for international line-haul work, generally consisting of a rigid truck towing a full trailer, an arrangement which gives them the flexibility of being able to operate the truck on remote internal routes also.

During the long snow-covered winters, followed by muddy conditions in early spring, many routes have even lower axle-load limits to prevent heavy trucks from damaging the frost-beaten surfaces. Many heavy trucks are fitted with double-drive bogies to improve traction in bad conditions, and some truckers carry a set of snowchains all year round to conquer the steep grades during heavy snow or rain which can turn the roads into muddy tracks. Gravel holders are also frequently fitted in front of the driving wheels, to spray sand or gravel on slippery inclines.

Norwegian truckers often prefer to drive at night because there is less passenger traffic on the road, and because the big trucks – with a whole battery of driving- and marker-lights at front and rear – are more easily spotted at night by oncoming vehicles and someone can pull off the road in time. (Most routes are not wide enough to allow two big trucks to pass each other.) In many parts of Norway owner-operators have joined forces and formed transport groups or companies comprising both passenger and goods vehicles and serving the many small townships in a large area all the year round. Several goods and passenger combined vehicles are

2

3

1

1. *Norway has a large fleet of trucks which operate internationally.*

2. *This DAF FT2200 of Majorstua has its sleeper compartment in the front of the trailer.*

3. *A Danish-operated Scania 141.*

4. *Finnish-built Sisu being loaded in typical Arctic-circle weather.*

4

employed throughout northern Scandinavia for operation to the more remote places. Most of these are built on coach chassis, up to 12.5 m length in the case of Norway.

A rigid truck and full trailer can measure up to 18 m under Norwegian legislation. While rigid two- and three-axle trucks and four- or five-axle drawbars make up the bulk of the vehicles in use, a number of derivations have developed particularly suited to narrow mountain road operation. Heavy three-axle double-drive tractors coupled to short single-axle semi-trailers perform well on twisting fjord-roads in all weathers, and so do rigid six-wheelers pulling heavy single-axle loaded trailers – of those several are of mixed construction for combined, fuel or dry commodity cargoes. In addition a fair number of coach-based pantechnicons are operated, which will give an improved ride for both the driver and goods on the corrugated roads.

Norway has no truck manufacturers of its own, and so all vehicles come from abroad. Scania and Volvo dominate, but Mercedes-Benz, DAF, MAN, Magirus-Deutz, Bedford, Leyland and Ford are also represented, and a number of Macks are in operation, but mainly on heavy haulage work. All these trucks have to earn respect the hard way, as they work through the long dark winter, lasting from late October until April. Many trucks – sometimes even buses – are mobilized for snow-clearing in badly affected areas. For this function a large number of vehicles are already equipped with a snowplough attachment, and along many routes rows of waiting v-shaped snowploughs are strategically placed and maintained by the government roadcrews.

Though new bridges are built regularly all over Norway to span fjords and lakes, many of these waters still have to be crossed by ferry – another obstacle for the truck operations, particularly during the long queues of the holiday season. Fortunately for the Norwegian trucker the rule is that commercial traffic gets priority at all times.

There is proportionally little road transport between Scandinavian countries, though Norwegians have a large number of trucks on long-distance international hauls and some even make regular trips from Oslo to Pakistan.

Finland's truckers undertake the long hauls too, and many Europeans are familiar with the name Polar Express, a company which operates hun-

dreds of big trucks to every destination in Europe and far beyond into the Middle East, and has many affiliated hauliers and depots in other countries. Obviously for TIR type operations (when vehicles are sealed by Customs at the start of their trip and are not re-examined by frontier officials until they reach their destination) tractor-semi-trailer and draw-bar outfits of 38 tonnes gross and within 18 m length predominate to comply with various foreign legislation, but since 1 July 1975 maximum dimensions and capacities for commercial vehicles in Finland itself have been stepped up considerably. Following the very liberal regulations on truck weight and length in neighbouring Sweden the Finnish authorities now allow a rigid truck of 12 m, a tractor-semi-trailer up to 20 m and a truck-draw-bar-trailer combination to be 22 m in length, however within a 42 tonne overall gcw and single axle at 10 or bogie at 16 tonnes. By liberal regulations such as these the Finnish haulier operating a maximum permitted outfit can now achieve an energy saving of almost 20 per cent per tonne payload compared with a British 32 tonner. This certainly makes trucking far more profitable up north where distances are long and road and weather conditions harsh.

Finland is not nearly as mountainous as Norway and has very long stretches of desolate highways of good standard; in the more remote northern places, however, there is little point in improving the earth tracks as very few vehicles use them daily. Owing to the hard operating conditions trucks have to be of tough, good quality and must be maintained thoroughly. To help ensure this Finland has built some of its own vehicles. Vanaja started with building 4×4 trucks for the Finnish army during World War II in association with Sisu; however this collaboration did not last long and in 1948 the companies went separate ways. Vanaja ventured farther afield in the all-wheel-drive category which was their speciality, using AEC or Leyland engines for their bonneted models (which proved popular in the difficult logging operations of inner Finland). Until absorbed again by Sisu in 1967, Vanaja produced a range of conventional and cabover models, the latter with the Leyland Ergomatic cab and diesel engines of 234 hp coupled to Fuller eight-speed gearboxes. Many of these sturdy vehicles are still in daily use – not only in Finland, for several were exported to Spain,

This tanker outfit operated by Shell is an R-series Sisu. Power for the range of conventional four- and six-wheeler vehicles is supplied by either Leyland or Rolls-Royce diesel engines. Gearbox is a Fuller and axles are by Sisu.

Venezuela, Argentina and Asia.

Sisu began production in 1931 and manufactured various models from 3 to 6 tons before the first Vanaja merger and wartime building of army trucks, but after the war the company proceeded alone to develop their K and L types with a 140 hp diesel for the heaviest 8.5 tonner. Later models were fitted with Leyland diesels of up to 210 hp in both conventional and cabover chassis, and a number of these were exported too. In 1973 new conventional L and R series trucks and tractors were available with 170 or 250 hp Leyland diesels in the two-axle models, and for the heavier three-axle vehicle types Rolls-Royce Eagle engines up to 335 hp with Fuller nine-speed gearboxes could be specified. The cabover M161 or M162 fitted with either the 265 hp Leyland 690 or the 275 hp Rolls-Royce diesel were still offered, and a heavier Eagle diesel of 320 hp is also available now. Alongside these genuine Finnish products there are many Volvo and Scania trucks in operation, and increasing numbers of other European makes are marketed, among which the various Mercedes-Benz, MAN, Magirus-Deutz, DAF, Bedford, and

Ford models can be observed, plus a few Japanese trucks in the medium-duty class.

In Denmark the truck scene is more akin to West European operations. Virtually all big truck names sell here, to comply with limitations of 38 tonnes and 18 m maximum length. British manufacturers do well too and many Leyland, Ford or Bedford trucks (including heavy TM types) have found favour in Denmark – another Scandinavian country with a long list of operators working international runs and gruelling Asian trails. Denmark does not house any truck manufacturers of her own, but Danish trucks are easily distinguished by their neat well-maintained bodywork in gleaming red, blue or white paint. Many draw-bar outfits engaged on long-distance fish-haulage stand apart for their beautiful appearance and cleanliness.

SWEDEN

Over 70 per cent of Swedish truck firms are owner-operated. Sweden is of course the homeland both of Volvo and Scania trucks, whose sales growth can be attributed to their excellent specification and ruggedness, developed in the harsh conditions found in their native land, a land often covered with freezing snow. Without doubt Scania and Volvo have been trend-setters in world trucking since the mid-1960s, bringing new dimensions to the market with their 'off the shelf' high-gross-weight and brute-horsepower trucks.

Much of this high specification comes from the liberal Swedish gross weight and vehicle length laws which allow, for instance, draw-bar rigs to be up to 24 m (approximately 78 ft) in length and to have a gross weight of some 51.4 metric tonnes on six axles.

Recently governing bodies concerned with road safety, and also those concerned with promoting the railway freight business, have been endeavouring to get the maximum vehicle length cut down from 24 m to 18 m on the grounds of increased road safety. It is argued that these lengthy combinations are a hazard to car drivers trying to pass them; argued against this is the fact that such a shortening of vehicle lengths would only bring more trucks to the roads to carry the same freight (and government figures reveal that of all accidents involving cars and trucks, just 6 per cent are as a result of overtaking collisions).

Since not all roads in Sweden can take really heavy trucks the Swedes have a two-class road system. The light road network allows axles up to 8 metric tonnes and bogies or tandems up to 12 combined tonnes, and this is called the 8/12 tonne road system. The heavy road system is built to handle the heaviest of Swedish truck combinations and allows for 10 tonne axles and 16 tonne tandems, and this is called the 10/16 tonne road system; some 90 per cent of Swedish highways are built to this heavier specification. In addition to the normal weight limits many roads in the north of Sweden are actually reclassed upwards – from 8/12 tonnes to 10/16 tonnes axle weight – during the freezing cold winters, when the ground becomes so cold and hard that it is able to withstand the weight increase.

It would not be possible, or financially sound practice, to build trucks with two different axle weight specifications, so Swedish manufacturers

1

2

1. Still in factory primer as it poses for the photographer, the Scania 146 bonneted tractor is powered by the 365 bhp V8 engine.

2. A Volvo F10 six-wheel tilt advances undeterred in typical Scandinavian conditions.

3. An example of the Volvo F12 tractor unit coupled to tri-axle tilt semi as often used for TIR work. The F12 was successor to the F89.

build their trucks to the higher axle weight, and operators simply load the vehicles less heavily when travelling over the 8/12 tonne road system. Trucks found violating these weight limits – especially if running above the 8/12 tonne limit on the light-weight road system – bring down a very heavy fine on the head of the vehicle operator. This fine can be in the region of 7,000–8,000 Swedish Kroner for the first offence, double that for a further offence.

No current figures are available, but at the end of 1975 there were some 150,000 trucks operating in Sweden, most of them built after 1968. The vast majority of all heavy trucks working in Sweden today are either Volvo or Scania; however there are around 3,000 American Chevrolet, International and Willys small vans and trucks, and some 30,000 medium-weight Mercedes and European-built Fords in use.

With the tough Swedish laws relating to cab strength there is little chance of any foreign heavy-weight trucks penetrating Sweden's home market, and these tough cab-strength laws have enabled both Volvo and Scania to earn their reputation for well-built cabs. Swedish cab-strength regulations are designed to give the driver the greatest possible protection inside his cab, ensuring that he will not be crushed or injured should the truck be involved in a collision, and that the cab doors will stay closed even in a bad crash. Three crushing tests are applied to every proposed new cab design for use in Sweden, and before the design can go into production it has to pass these tests.

The first test is to let a 1 metric tonne concrete block swing against the front windscreen pillar from a distance of 10 ft. For the second test a 1 tonne flat slab swings against the rear cab wall, again from a distance of 10 feet. As if that was not enough, a massive 15 tonne static load is then placed on the cab roof. If the cab can take all three punishments without undue buckling, and the cab doors stay shut, then it is passed for sale on the Swedish trucking market.

Truck drivers also come in for some tough driving tests in Sweden before they can take to the highway with a truck of their own. There are eight grades of driving licence, applying to vehicles ranging from a car to a multi-axle truck combination, and before taking any driving test the would-be driver has to prove that he has undergone the man-

The Volvo range of bonneted models embraces N7, N10 and N12 models with 6.7, 9.6 and 12 litre engines respectively. Pictured here is a six-wheeled N7 vacuum tanker.

datory ten to thirteen weeks minimum driving instruction.

The Swedish railway system plays a large part in the movement of freight within Sweden, and the basic formula is for the railways to carry long-distance freight and the trucks to carry the local and short-haul freight. An average of 80 per cent of all truck miles are on short-distance work. It is an odd fact that the largest of the few trucking fleets in Sweden is owned by Swedish State Railways.

Sweden is undoubtedly a land of owner-drivers, and the vast majority of operators run just one truck. The 19,000 operators running heavy-weight equipment own just 37,000 trucks, with a mere 5 per cent of operators owning more than five trucks. The owner-drivers do not contract themselves out individually or go looking for work for their one truck only, as is common practice for owner-drivers in most other countries; instead, they combine to form 'Centralls'.

These Centralls operate on the basis of a large co-operative company where everyone has a share of the business and profits proportional to the number of vehicles supplied, and so with a seemingly large combined fleet of trucks, the Centrall is able to undertake large bulk movements of freight and get good contracts, sharing the work and profits among its owner-driver members. Some large Centralls have management staffs appointed from their members and are also able to provide workshop facilities and buy diesel and oil for members in bulk.

HOLLAND

Despite the windmills, tulips and wooden shoes Holland is one of Europe's most industrialized and modern countries; the Flying Dutchman has become a trucker.

Dutch operators haul more than 40 per cent of all goods moving between EEC member countries. Holland climbed high up the road transport ladder following World War II, when the Allied forces abandoned huge quantities of army vehicles in Europe. The number of army truck dumps in Holland was in those days alarmingly great. The sums spent by transport operators making ex-army vehicles suitable for civilian use were enormous, while the mechanical condition, economic viability and spare parts availability of most vehicles left much to be desired. Nevertheless many US Army trucks like GMC, Mack, Reo and Diamond T were the basis of now successful truck operations.

Unlike the transport philosophies of other countries, road transport in Holland is being acknowledged and estimated as an independent, economically viable activity. Among other reasons this is because of the country's excellent position with regard to big harbours and industrial neighbouring countries: Holland has always been the gateway and distribution centre for Europe.

About 80 per cent of all goods transported go by truck; the remainder is divided between the railways and inland barges. Over 9,000 million tonne km is transported by large truck fleets; the rest by owner-operators. Over 60,000 heavy trucks are now registered in Holland, a country of only 14 million people. About 600 companies are operating more than fifteen trucks, among which there are many with fleets of a hundred vehicles or more.

Most cargoes transported by road in the Benelux countries (Belgium, the Netherlands, Luxembourg) are raw materials and related products, followed by foodstuffs as the next largest category. Most truck operators obtain their loads from manufacturers or through an agent (many of whom are settled at the port of Rotterdam). Dutch-registered long-distance trucks can be seen all over Europe, and even far beyond – in Saudi Arabia, Pakistan, Nigeria and the Soviet Union. Holland has an agreement with the USSR to carry out 500 trips a year but, due to the very competitive prices of the Russians, only the Russians themselves have been able to use such permits to the full. England – now in the EEC – has also become an important

destination for Dutch hauliers, but although the distance is relatively short, the ferry crossings can be time-consuming and costly. A typical Holland–Italy round-trip of 1,500 miles usually takes five or six days including delays at the borders, even with TIR coverage. Though crossing European borders is much easier nowadays, a lot of paper-work and checking must still be carried out, particularly for southern European destinations like Yugoslavia or Spain.

Although it is one of the smallest countries in Europe Holland has a very advanced system of modern highways. Being a low country, with much land reclaimed from the sea, it still has one of the highest permitted gross weights of Europe, allowing a six-axle rig to gross at 50 tons. However, this mass must be within an 18 m overall length limit for a truck and full trailer combination or a 15.5 m long articulated set-up, except for the recently permitted 'double bottom' combinations consisting of a two-axle tractor pulling a single-axle semi to which another two-axle full trailer is coupled. These are generally of 18 m length. However, with a special permit it is quite easy to extend semi-trailer lengths to as much as 24 m, and many operators with extendable trailers carrying steel or concrete girders can be seen on major highways in between other heavies.

Axle weights are 10 tonnes for a single and 16 tonnes for a bogie, but this will be increased to 18 tonnes soon. Recent developments on the Dutch roads include many eight-wheeled rigids with a 32 tonne gvw for hauling concrete, bulk fuel or sand and bricks, plus a number of these twin-steer rigids pulling full trailers to carry 20 ft containers. Of course, many of these heavy trucks can only operate legally within Dutch boundaries and have a 38 tonne limit for international hauls to Germany or Belgium. The speed limit for trucks in Holland is 80 km per hour, but most trucks are geared for higher speeds and actually cruise at 90 to 100 km per hour without too much trouble from local police so long as the trucker does not obstruct or endanger other road users.

A driver needs a 'C' licence to drive a truck over 3.5 tons, but this C licence includes automatically a 'D' licence (for buses) and an 'E' licence (for trailers). Anyone over eighteen years of age may apply for a truck driving test, but recently more stringent regulations have been introduced which require that young professional truckers up to twenty-three (shortly to be twenty-five) years of age must attend courses at trucking schools, where, in addition to driving techniques and traffic regulations, they learn diesel mechanics and paper-work.

Trucking in Holland – as in many other countries – means a hard fight for survival for both operator and driver, and most work sixty or more hours a week. This has now become more difficult to do, however, since all trucks over 3.5 tons are now compulsorily fitted with tachographs, recording instruments which register driving and rest periods. A trucker driving in Holland can still clock up an eleven-hour driving day, but this is to be reduced to ten hours during 1979, and on international runs the eight-hour EEC limit applies. Before the tachograph ruling came into effect early in 1975 thousands of angry truckers blocked the thirty-five main border-crossing points of Holland and Germany/Belgium, and even the ferry-crossing points to England, for two days in December 1974. The tachographs were bitterly opposed by the carriers of fruit and flowers, who have tight schedules to maintain because of the perishable nature of their cargoes. It is not only the truck operators, however, who have to comply with various regulations, for manufacturers of commercial vehicles are also plagued with new limits on noise levels and smoke emission.

Holland has only one truck manufacturer of international repute – DAF – who began in 1928 building trailer equipment and later developed and produced army truck components such as additional axles, winches and drive-assemblies. Actual vehicle production started in the early 1950s with medium-weight cabover trucks and tractors. Today DAF manufacture trucks and tractors and a whole range of semi- and full trailers in all weight categories up to 50 tons, using their own diesel engines from 100 to 325 bhp. Fuller nine- or thirteen-speed gearboxes are now offered on the heaviest 2800 range, perhaps due to the tie-up with the Americans at International Harvester (who have a one-third stake in the company). Up to now only a few DAF 2200 tractors have been shipped to the United States, but IH sells several heavy DAF models under its own name, in South Africa for example. DAF aims to produce 15,000 trucks in 1979, about half of them exported.

Another Dutch manufacturer of heavy trucks is Floor at Hilversum, who produce FTF trucks and tractors in the top weight category, as well as building trailers. In fact Floor, too, started life as a trailer manufacturer but began assembling Mack trucks in 1952 for the Benelux countries. In 1964 Mack decided to discontinue the agreement with Floor and set up their own distribution arrangements for Europe. FTF trucks were hence born to replace the Macks, many of the early home-bred models featuring leftover Mack engines and axles. FTF trucks today are custom-built, with Detroit diesel-power and Fuller or Allison gearboxes.

2

1. *This particular Flying Dutchman is a model 1626 Mercedes-Benz powered by a 260 bhp V8 engine and operated by a northern Holland haulier.*

2. *Because of the liberal gross weight regulations in the Netherlands there is an increase in the number of vehicles built to take advantage of them, and this Mack timber hauler is a typical example, though it is not as popular with operators as the locally built trucks. By adopting a six axle configuration, gross weights up to 50 tonnes are obtainable.*

1

Many are used for heavy haulage operations, though others using the 8V–71N or newer 8V–92T coupled to Fuller thirteen-speed gearb6xes are ideally suited to maximum-weight road haulage or even TIR work abroad. The FTF cab, incidentally, is a British Motor Panels design similar to ERF 'European' and Guy 'Big J' sleepers.

In addition to DAF and FTF Holland has some smaller truck manufacturers like Terberg, Ginaf and RAM who specialize in building off-road vehicles and a few highway models, all from ex-army components. Most of these are of American origin with Reo or Diamond T chassis, axles, springs, etc. but they are now used together with new DAF, Volvo or Mercedes-Benz diesel engines and self-made or modified factory cabs. These trucks are moderately priced and are often reliable strong workhorses, particularly popular with small private tipper operators.

The most interesting Dutch truck from the past was the quality Kromhout. The factory started in 1935 building Gardner engines under licence and soon fitted them to their own truck and bus chassis. After World War II Kromhout manufactured a whole range of very strong two- and three-axle trucks and tractors with both Gardner and 200 hp Rolls-Royce diesels, but the company merged with Verheul in 1961. Verheul produced its own trucks and buses using both Kromhout and AEC components until 1965. It later formed the basis for Leyland in Holland.

Despite a relatively small market almost all European manufacturers compete in Holland today and American Mack, White, Autocar and even Oshkosh try to get a hold, but only Mack has succeeded with 600 trucks imported yearly. Maybe these US rigs have started the now increasing cult of fitting out Dutch rigs with chromed bumpers, airhorns and lots of markerlights and fancy paint schemes, giving both the driver and owner more pride in their vehicles.

Wooden or steel sided bodies and tilt or closed van-type trucks and trailers are most used in Holland. Open flat-bed vehicles are not favoured because of rainy weather and pilfering, plus the fact that a Dutchman does not like to get his hands dirty roping and sheeting huge loads after just a short hop around the country, for Holland is so small that a trucker pushing hard can drive twice round the country in one day!

1

2

3

4

1. The FTF has been successful in the 'heavy' market.

2. Although a typical long-distance outfit the Mack is not often seen in this rôle.

3. This multi-axle Volvo drawbar outfit can gross up to 50 tonnes in Holland.

4. The twin-steer variety of tractors were popular during the 1960s.

BELGIUM AND FRANCE

For very many years there has been a wide choice of commercial vehicles, from both local and foreign manufacturers, in Belgium and France, although in Belgium the emphasis nowadays is mainly on imports. France, on the contrary, produces very many trucks but, due to mergers and bankruptcies, several well-known makes have disappeared in the last ten years.

In Belgium, from 1911, the firm Miesse offered small commercial vehicles, and ten years later the company produced heavy trucks with six- or eight-cylinder engines of 100 hp. These petrol engines were followed in 1932 by Gardner diesels built under licence (a similar arrangement to that of Kromhout in Holland). Miesse trucks were always remarkable for their unusual axle set-ups or cab constructions; even rigid eight-wheelers were produced. After World War II several types of cabover and conventional trucks were offered with Gardner 6LX or 6LXB diesels, and the latest models of 1968 had Detroit 6V-53N diesel engines coupled to six-speed ZF gearboxes. Besides these there were some models marketed with German Bussing engines.

Another Belgian manufacturer who ceased truck production was Brossel, who had been selling heavy trucks with their own diesel engines and other components made in their own workshops since the early 1930s. After the war Brossel conventional models were fitted with Leyland 0.600 diesels of 125 hp coupled to a six-speed gearbox and capable of hauling a 27 ton gcw combination. However, Brossel soon became Leyland Motors Belgium and specialized in the production of buses. The third extinct name is FN, who primarily built 4×4 trucks with petrol engines for the Belgian army, but some chassis were also available for civilian use. It is unfortunate that there was a steady disappearance of so many well-built trucks, but a few examples of the types can still be seen working in Belgium today, notably around the Antwerp docks shunting heavy loads over short distances.

The only present-day truck manufactured completely in Belgium is MOL, who started building trailers and truck bodies after World War II, but added heavy truck models to the range in the 1960s. In addition to its trailers MOL specializes in the building of oilfield vehicles, tippers, heavy haulage tractors and crane carriers in various weight categories. In 1969 both a bonneted and cabover 6×4 or 6×6 chassis for tipper work was marketed, fitted with an eight-cylinder air-cooled Deutz diesel of 230 hp and six-speed ZF gearbox. These types HF and F2664/2666 had a gross vehicle weight of 26 tons or a train-weight of 40 tons.

Newer vehicles include the HFT 644, a 6.5 ton gvw off-highway oilfield truck, and the bigger HFT 1066 and HFT 2666 6×6 drive conventionals for tipper or concrete-mixer operation. But certainly the most impressive model is the huge T 6066 6×6 heavy haulage tractor with a Deutz turbo-charged V-12 air-cooled diesel of nearly 400 hp driving through a Clark power-shift transmission with eight speeds and torque converter. Maximum gcw is up to 260 tonnes on-highway or 130 tonnes off the road. With the 38 tonne gross limit in Belgium these vehicles can only be operated with special permits, but are developed primarily for the export market.

With length limits of 15 m for a tractor-semi-trailer and 18 m for a draw-bar outfit, the vehicles in Belgium do not differ much from their European counterparts, with the exception of Britain and Holland. The majority of vehicles consist of a two- or three-axle truck or tractor pulling a two-axle trailer and closed van, TIR tilt or dropside bodies being favoured above flat-beds. However, unlike other European countries, conventional model tractors or trucks make up the larger proportion of the vehicles, while cabovers are more generally engaged on international runs.

Many trucks from the past can still be seen jolting over cobbled streets or concrete highways and, apart from the Belgian extinct makes mentioned above, aged Bussing, Krupp, AEC, Mack and even Reo, White and Brockway trucks are still making money after many a mile. New imports include almost all European manufacturers, but also some Japanese Hino and Nissan, plus big US White, Mack and Autocar heavies. Many big truck manufacturers have set up assembly plants in Belgium: Bedford, Mack, Hino, Volvo and Pegaso, to name a few, though some are more successful than others. In addition many Belgian operators have fitted their own cabs and superstructures on factory chassis to give their vehicles personal identity, or to enlarge the cab interiors – a good example is the company of Camermans in Antwerp.

The biggest body and trailer manufacturer is undoubtedly Van Hool, who sell their premium equipment not only all over Europe but have many ties with African and Asian countries. The firm is well known for its range of modern city and line buses and distinguished luxury coaches.

In mid-1978 many Antwerp dock-workers held up hundreds of fuel tanker trucks, in particular at the Dutch and French borders, to avoid these bringing fuel to Belgian filling stations, which were laid dry due to strikes at the refineries. Many truckers suffered when over-heated workers molested drivers and smashed up windshields, mirrors and tyres in an attempt to prevent truckers from delivering the badly needed fuel.

Belgium is, however, generally a quiet trucking country, and there is not such a strong anti-truck feeling from government and public as in *la douce France*. Transport operators here are accorded strong opposition from Paris and the media, while the French railways are heavily subsidized and still favoured as the future of goods transport. But French manufacturers have to admit that goods are far more efficiently handled by road transport, and

An older type of bonneted Scania Vabis seen alongside a Brussels tramcar during the 1960s. It was this type of Scania truck which did much to enhance the prestige of Swedish trucks abroad.

an increase in truck traffic is unavoidable with the fluctuations in the economy. Already trucks make up the greater part of the traffic on many routes in France; even at weekends hundreds of heavy rigs mix with other vehicles. Some truckers take wife and children along on long cross-country hauls, which can last up to four days, since from north to south is a 1,000 km haul.

During the last ten years France has constructed several hundred miles of divided highway of very modern lay-out, but because these are all toll-roads, and certainly not cheap, the majority of truckers prefer to drive the *routes nationales* which wind from one place to another and are generally of three-lane construction. During the summer months in particular, when tens of thousands of tourists pack the main north–south toll-highways, truckers fare better on secondary roads or driving

1

3

2

1. AEC trucks were once popular in Belgium, as shown by these Mogul tractors seen coupled to tankers of British beer at the quayside.

2. Right up to its demise in 1970 the French Willème still sported the American Liberty badge which originated in the 1914–18 war. Here an example pulls out of the docks at Rouen.

3. Belgian-registered Volvo N720 tractor with tank semi-trailer. Where overall length is not at a premium, many drivers prefer the comfort of a conventional unit with its roomier cab.

4. Situated at the crossroads of Europe, Belgium has long been an open market for all comers, especially in recent years with all home production at an end. Even so, it is unusual to find the Lancia 'Esagamma' tucked away in an alley.

5. Drawbar outfits are unusual in France, although this 1960s Saviem with its load of waste paper is outside one of the by no means unusual cafés!

4

5

on through the night. As in many other countries around the world these caravan-towing and sight-seeing sun-seekers are a menace to the professional driver, not only holding up traffic but parking their cars on truck-stop carparks, leaving the truck driver no choice but to push on to the next over-crowded area. As in Belgium, there is not much variety in truck configurations in France, which has an overall length for a semi-trailer outfit of 15 m and for a truck-trailer of 18 m, plus a maximum weight limit of 38 tonnes gcw, but with a 13 tonne axle allowance. Thus most of the vehicles are of a single drive axle type pulling a two- or three-axle bogie semi-trailer, with far less truck and full trailer combinations to be seen than in neighbour-ing countries. However, a few small 'double bottom' outfits are operated on designated routes for inter-city delivery work.

Trailers are almost invariably made by Fruehauf or Trailor, and the tilt TIR type semi with three-axle single tyred bogie is seen most and is used for both domestic or international haulage. Not many old trucks are around these days, but France has produced a lot of interesting makes in the past, such as the renowned Bernard. Starting as a tipper manufacturer in 1924 Camions Bernard moved up through small 4- and 5-tonners in 1929 to big 10- and 12-ton trucks by 1939, in which Gardner diesels were fitted, once more built under licence. Heavy two- and three-axle trucks and tractors were announced in 1954 and these vehicles had double-reduction rear axles mounted in the chassis cross-members, while the power came from Bernard 120 or 150 hp diesels. Later, in 1960, a cabover of very modern appearance with 185 hp six-cylinder diesel and 12-speed gearbox was introduced in addition to a bonneted range of trucks and tractors for gross weights up to 35 tons. Most unusual for France were the Bernard cabover eight-wheelers with air suspension built for a big French meat haulier. Production ceased in 1966 when Mack took over the premises for its own vehicle assembly, but before that a number of heavy Bernards were pro-duced fitted with Mack diesels and other running parts. Only very few of these legendary French vehicles, which were advanced for the time, sur-vive today.

Latil is another distinct old name in the French trucking world, best known for its heavy haulage over-the-road tractors, with front- or all-wheel drive. Latil also manufactured a range of two- and three-axle truck chassis through the years, in both conventional and cabover form, and powered again by Gardner engines built under licence, with ratings up to 150 hp in the late 1950s. Afterwards the Latil name disappeared, when the company became part of Saviem, who are in turn part of the big Renault group (also comprising Berliet).

The name Renault has been well known in the automobile field for a very long time, but as early as World War I petrol-powered Renault trucks, distinguished by their sloping hoods, transported supplies to the battlefields. In 1934 a six-cylinder diesel truck with double-reduction rear axle, and a double-drive three-axle rigid for a 15 tonne payload were launched. Renault also ventured into the cabover field at this time, and new models appeared just before World War II. After 1945 emphasis lay on light- and medium-capacity trucks, but soon the Saviem range of heavier types was developed. Saviem was in fact the extension of Renault, Latil and Somua, who merged in the mid-1950s. Gradually the Saviem nameplates appeared on all heavy Renault Group vehicles, but in the late 1960s Saviem in its turn sought contact with MAN and Alfa-Romeo, leading to new developments at both ends of the light, medium and heavy truck ranges. Saviem's newest heavy trucks in the SM range still have many MAN components, but a re-styled cab and the Club of Four light- and medium-duty chassis, developed jointly with DAF, Magirus-Deutz and Volvo, have now been extended to include heavy 30-tonners in the P and N series. Power up to 320 hp comes from MAN, while in the lower class Perkins or Renault engines are fitted. Before joining the Renault group in 1955 Somua was well known for its Lanova powered trucks of the 1930s with 10- to 13-ton capacities, and gas-generator-powered trucks, produced around the time of World War II, proved well-built; but after issuing some more cabover tractor and truck chassis, again with Lanova diesels, right up into the 35-ton gcw bracket, production ceased around 1960.

Berliet has always been an important name on the French transport scene, and like Renault it was during World War I that the 4-ton CBA type Berliet trucks became famous. Models up to 7.5 tonnes followed, until in 1931 the first diesel-powered trucks were built. Before World War II heavy

truck chassis of 22 and even 28 tonnes gross were manufactured, and in 1946 production resumed with both bonneted and forward-control tilt-cab models. In 1955 the heavy TLM series with 200 hp six-cylinder diesel for a gross train weight of 35 tonnes found ready acceptance with many French hauliers. Another new series of cabovers and conventionals was born in 1959, of which several still survive. Today Berliet produces a vast line of light to heavy tractors and trucks, the top model in the highway section being the cabover TRH 350 with a Maxi-couple 350 hp V8 diesel driving through a Fuller thirteen-speed transmission. For a long time Berliet was the leader in huge oilfield tractors with engines up to 600 hp, but having supplied the Middle East and North Africa with hundreds of these specialized bonneted vehicles, mostly with 6×6 drive and capable of hauling loads of up to 250 tons across virgin desert, production was discontinued gradually due to tremendous development costs and relatively limited sales. Only a few conventional heavy 6×4 or 6×6 models are still built for heavy haulage purposes.

Another French manufacturer specializing in this field was Willème, now handled by Perez-Raimond in Paris, but dating back to the early days after World War I when the US-produced Liberty trucks were rebuilt and sold as 5-tonners. Production was concentrated on heavy vehicles right from the start, and many early three-axle trucks, France's first, were exported. In the 1930s heavy tractors joined the production lines. Willème manufactured its own diesels in those days and offered engines up to 260 hp for special applications. Besides these, heavy haulage rigs for a gcw of up to 110 tons were completely custom-built, and a few years later highway trucks and tractors up to 15 tonnes gvw or 35 tonnes gcw were introduced.

After the war a new range of highway models appeared, with the biggest being a double-drive three-axle 15 tonner with an eight-cylinder 225 hp diesel. Other time-improved models of the former type were introduced in 1953, with both cabover and conventional models being available. In addition the supply position on the African continent was improved by marketing specially designed oilfield equipment, the W8 SA model still being used throughout Algeria to carry huge indivisible loads. Due to an agreement with AEC in the early 1960s, when the British firm was trying to get a

1

2

*1. With Hazchem plate well to the fore a
French-registered Volvo N10 pulls on to the
autoroute on the outskirts of Paris.*

*2. Unic have been building trucks since 1908 and
were the first company to build a wholly French
diesel truck in 1930.*

foothold in Europe, Willème trucks underwent a
change, with unusual cab designs and the option of
AEC diesel engines and other AEC components.
The latest cabs for both the cabover and conventional models were made by Pelpel with very modern styling and either Willème or AEC diesels up to
280 hp fitted. Today power for various Willème
models offered by Perez-Raimond comes from
Detroit Diesel and covers the 8V–71N in the highway and tipper chassis, to the 16V–71N of 520 hp
in the huge four-axle TG 300 heavy-haulage tractor
for an amazing 1,000 tonnes gcw rig. Furthermore
Raimond developed a more modern extension of
the successful off-highway oilfield tractor, and this

type W8 SA.AR 6×6 is powered by an 8V–71
Detroit of 350 hp coupled to a Fuller thirteen-
speed box for gcw up to 75 tonnes.

Obviously, many of these extra-heavy vehicles
are seldom seen in Western Europe, but are of
prime importance in oil-producing countries.
Since Berliet ceased production of specialized
heavy tractors, Willème's enormous products have
taken over in the French heavy haulage field, and
from time to time gigantic vessels or transformers
can be seen transported on multi-wheeled Nicolas
trailers pulled and pushed by two TG 200 or 300
tractors – which will beat everything in power and
size on the French roads today.

To stay with the heavy-weights, the last name
which comes to mind is the Unic, which was built
from 1920 onwards in the light- to medium-weight
classes, but in the early 1930s trucks with their own
constructed diesels were offered in the heavier
category up to 15 tonnes payload. In 1946 the
long-nosed ZU range with set back front axle and
120 hp six-cylinder diesel fitted to the top end of
the range set new standards in French truck
design. Even longer bonneted models and new
cabovers appeared in 1955 with increased power
for the ZU range at 180 hp maximum. In the 1960s
modern aerodynamic tilt cabs were introduced for
the whole range, with the biggest engine option
being a V8 diesel of 270 hp. As part of Fiat since
1967, and now under the wing of the huge Iveco
concern, Unic's later cabover models all featured
Fiat cabs and other running parts of the group,
while for the heaviest trucks and tractors its own
V8 340 hp diesel is retained.

With such a wide choice of locally built vehicles
on offer, the French hauliers had little intention of
buying foreign, but today imports like Volvo,
Scania, DAF, Mercedes and Leyland are regularly
seen, while to a lesser extent Mack, Pegaso,
Magirus-Deutz and Ford are represented. In the
middle-weight class Bedford TK and Ford
D-series have a fair share of the market. One of the
few countries on the continent where ERF is selling reasonably well is France, and the same can be
said of Leyland with their Marathon.

Most heavy trucks in France are semi-trailer
outfits of plain appearance – except for the very
smart and clean refrigerated trucks frequently seen
at the end of the weekends bringing meat and other
perishable foodstuffs to Paris, Lyon or Marseille.

SPAIN AND PORTUGAL

The trucking industry in Spain is one of striking contrasts. The little four-wheeler pre-war Ford or Studebaker found in major centres contrasts sharply with the massive eight-wheeler Pegaso as each goes about its daily task, and the flamboyant colours of the trucks themselves stand out pleasingly against the azure Mediterranean or the bleached mountain regions.

Contradictions follow close upon contrasts in this exciting country. For instance, while the driving test for truck drivers is supposed to be the most difficult in the world, the standard of driving is frequently described as suicidal. Then, while Trabosa – a Spanish trailer builder – make some of the world's biggest trailers, Spain does not have a truck builder capable of producing a truck to pull them. Other anomalies include owner-drivers who install Telma retarders on their trailers, rather than tractors like the rest of the world, and the practice of Pegaso, the leading truck builder, who continued to build spherical air reservoirs when everyone else had long before opted for cylindrical. Add these many contrasts and contradictions to the beauty of the country and it is easily understood why Spain fascinates the road transport enthusiast and trucker alike.

There is a special quality to the sound of the industry in Spain too, a sound made up of endless gear-shifts on never-ending hills and of barking exhaust notes which are peculiar to Pegasos, Barreiros and Spanish-built Leyland trucks. But, more specifically, what most characterize Spanish trucking and the type of truck employed there are the weights hauled by these machines.

The difference, of course, lies in the fact that the rigid is found in far greater numbers than the articulated, a situation which exists for several reasons. The first is that weights for the biggest examples of both types of vehicle – the four-axle rigid and four-axle artic – are very similar. Second, a great deal of haulage inside the country is carried out by owner-operators who undoubtedly appreciate the additional safety afforded by twin-steer axles. And third, because the era of articulation has yet to be widely accepted, there is little advantage in operating a fleet of tractor-trailers if interchangeability is limited to a few other fleets in the country.

Unlike other West European countries road transport is the only way of moving goods reliably and fast within Spain, where the railways are of little importance for handling freight and waterways are unheard of, except for a few small coastal container lines. A visitor to Spain is immediately struck by the enormous amount of commercial vehicles on the endless highways which cross the country from one side to the other. These roads are usually of good single-lane construction, but toll-highways have recently been built connecting major cities, and catering primarily for the great numbers of tourists who flock to the eastern Mediterranean coast. However, as in France, most truckers prefer the old toll-free highways where the local cafés give them an enjoyable break, and in any case the Spanish trucker – often an owner-operator – is not as hard-pressed as his more northern counterparts to get to his destination in the shortest possible time.

As mentioned, main country highways are of a good standard, often with a third lane to allow faster traffic to overtake the generously loaded heavy trucks. Because of the extreme summer heat several major highways have damaged surfaces with deep ruts in the soft bitumen, and extremely corrugated stretches of highway are found on higher inland plains, though they are still named E highways. Many high mountain ranges are scattered over the Spanish peninsula and provide really tough tests for heavy highway trucks, which can gross 38 tonnes gcw maximum within a length limit of 16.50 m for an articulated rig, and 18.00 m for a drawbar combination. To make mountain driving safer and less tiresome, big trucks and artics are often equipped with Telma retarders built behind the gearbox or in the differential or on a trailer. These consist of electrically operated magnetos giving great retardation on the driven axle. Most Spanish trucks sport an abundance of colourful paint and bolt-on goodies such as chrome spotlights, air-horns and other gadgets fitted both inside and out, giving the trucks a very distinctive look.

It is not only the new trucks which make the colourful scene, for most owner-operators keep their vehicles in immaculate condition for many years and it is not rare even today to see trucks built in the 1930s and 1940s still operating successfully, especially in the light- to medium-duty field. But how long this will be the case, as prices continue to rise steadily and most hauliers have to compete

hard to survive, is debatable. A comparison between the number of old trucks on Spanish roads in 1978 and the figure, say, five years previously shows a big reduction, and the day is not far off when the sole trucks on the road will be either new Barreiros (Chrysler-Dodge España) or Pegaso, with a number of the lighter Ebro and Avia, and a handful of foreign imports. Obviously many small hauliers tend to hold on to their faithful old beasts as long as possible, which is a fairly long time since rust problems are not acute in the fine sunny weather and very low humidity; and besides prices of new vehicles are almost prohibitive. The beautiful 1950s-style Leyland Beavers and Super Beavers are still seen today, as well as the smaller Comets – all great bonneted models manufactured for many years under licence and proudly displaying the badge 'El Camion Ingles'. In addition a number of old Mercedes, MAN and ÖAF together with a few American heavies survive, but the majority of trucks these days are from the latest Spanish model ranges.

Pegaso trucks started life in the former Hispano-Suiza plant around 1946, using many

Because of the better climate, trucks do not rust away as they do in damper zones. A 1941 Ford of typical Spanish style rumbles along past the more modern Pegaso twin-steer in the background.

Leyland parts, but producing its own 100-hp six-cylinder diesel for cabover trucks with an 8-ton capacity (many of these are still in daily use). This first range was followed by the very futuristic pressed-steel cabover of 1956, which is still marketed, with minor modifications to the original design and with technically up-to-date components, as a tipper and mixer chassis. These aerodynamically shaped sleeper-cab models, designated the 1063, 1066, 1080 and 2011 series, had engines up to 260 hp and are a frequent sight on the European international highways, even in 1979. Pegaso now produces over 26,000 vehicles a year, from small Sava vans to 50-ton gcw tractors and trucks, of which the 2180–2189 series is top of the range with modern tilt short- or sleeper-cabs, and diesels up to 352 hp coupled to Fuller nine-speed gearboxes. In addition to a number of well penetrated European markets Pegaso is a successful contender in most of Latin-America.

Barreiros SA of Madrid entered the truck manufacturing business in 1951 in collaboration with AEC, and gradually built up a good business in direct competition with Pegaso. Early vehicles had cabs using Berliet pressings (and perhaps other components). The earliest model was a four-wheel cabover followed later by both forms of six wheeler – regular and the twin-steer 'Chinese Six' variety. It was unfortunate that for very many years no rigid eight-wheeler was available from the factory, with the result that the market was taken largely by Pegaso, for Barreiros customers had to rely on dealer-added axles. As with Pegaso, it was many years before Barreiros introduced a tilt-cab, a feature which is almost mandatory these days.

Anxious to expand their European sales, Chrysler succeeded in gradually acquiring large shares in Barreiros, until in 1967 they had a controlling interest and the company became Chrysler España. Some of the smaller Dodge commercials of US design were added to the range, and were for a while labelled Barreiros. A completely new style of cab for the heavy range was introduced in 1976, and the Barreiros name continued until 1978 when it was dropped in favour of Dodge for all vehicles in the Chrysler Europe range – another move deplored by truck enthusiasts. Top of the range at present is the 37 tonne gross 84/37B rigid eight-wheeler powered by a 300 hp job, and this chassis is extensively used for this legal weight in Spain.

Next comes the 26 tonne gross twin-steer six-wheeler, followed by the smaller models in the range. The tractor version was the first model in the range to be marketed in Britain, as the maximum-capacity articulated unit for the UK Dodge line-up.

The third well-known Spanish manufacturer of trucks is Ebro, the majority of whose vehicles are sold in the light- to medium-duty field. Ebro actually started as a local Ford truck manufacturer as far back as 1920, with the last Ford Thames-based models coming off the production lines ten years ago. Many of these vehicles are still giving good performance in competition with newer Ebro E and P series trucks, the latter powered by the 6.354 or V8.540 Perkins diesels coupled to six-speed ZF synchromesh gearboxes and capable of hauling up to 27 tonnes gross for the P–190 tractor. Ebro trucks are also exported to over twenty countries world-wide.

Other Spanish-built vehicles still in existence, though no longer manufactured, include the Avia, Nazar and Karpetan. Inevitably, most of the European manufacturers are represented in Spain, but it is rather more difficult to explain the presence of marques such as Sisu from Finland, Fuso and Hino from Japan or Diamond T, Autocar and IHC from the United States. In the heavy haulage sector of the industry, rare types such as Kaelble, Hayes and Oshkosh are also seen, though this may be explained to some extent by the fact that neither Pegaso nor Barreiros produce a vehicle suitable for

The twin-steer six wheeler, often referred to as a Chinese six, has been very popular in the Iberian peninsula, perhaps for the greater safety attributed to two front axles on mountain roads.

An ÖAF 980 owned by an independent trucker leads a line of vehicles along a twisting Spanish mountain road. The ÖAF is successor to the AF or Austro Fiat trucks of the pre-war period.

extra-heavy haulage, and operators are thus forced to look outside Spain for such vehicles. Mack is far ahead in this field, marketing both conventional and cabover models, the latter F-model being the mainstay of the big fleet of Transportes San Jose at Renteria, one of the major Spanish international operating haulage firms. This company also has a number of R-series Macks with self-made sleeper extensions in use on their routes to most European cities. Other large fleet owners are, for example, Mateu and Mateu, Transportes Generales Martinez and Transdonat, all frequently seen abroad hauling fruits or machinery to keep the Spanish economy alive – and to show the world the beautifully decorated Pegaso and Barreiros trucks which typify the sunny Spanish trucking scene.

It is the interpretation of the axle weight laws, mentioned earlier, which has contributed most significantly to the type of vehicle found in Spain. Put in its simplest form, the law states that twin-tyre axles have a gross weight allowance of 10 tonnes and single-tyre axles a gross weight of 8.5 tonnes. This means that a four-wheeler may operate at 18.5 tonnes gvw (provided there are large enough tyres on the front axle), a 'Chinese Six' at 27 tonnes gross, an eight-wheeler at $35\frac{1}{2}$ tonnes gross and a four-axle artic at 38 tonnes gcw. It should be explained at this stage that most Spanish eight-wheelers employ a single-tyred axle (either steered or self-steering) as the fourth axle, and consequently one drive-axle only. Some double-drive rear-axle assemblies are seen, but these are generally installed on the on/off highway type of vehicles and not on highway rigs.

The Spanish owner-driver is a colourful character and this is reflected strongly in the decoration adorning the rig he drives. Vehicle exteriors are splashed with colour and most cabs are fitted with an exterior sun visor which carries the name of either the driver's wife or girl-friend, or perhaps the company he is sub-contracted to. Rather strangely, Scots tartans are very often seen adorning the interior of Spanish cabs, although leather-work is also popular. Pegaso produce some very expensive-looking wheel hub caps which depict Pegasus, the winged horse from which the company obviously takes its name, and although the Spanish manufacturers have not yet progressed to the stage where they offer chromed vertical exhaust stacks or polished aluminium fuel tanks, the driver compensates very adequately by improvising with individually styled pieces of metal or even name badges from another type of truck.

That drivers are not only concerned with the appearance of their trucks but also with their mechanical condition is evidenced by the fact that there are many exquisite examples of old vehicles operating in Spain. Ask a driver to show you the engine of his fifteen- or twenty-year-old Leyland (complete with third axle modification of course) and you will be shown a power plant clean enough to be in a vintage Bentley. And it is not uncommon to see the driver of a disabled truck carry out a complete repair at the roadside, often with the

For very many years the bonneted versions of the Leyland truck range were very popular in Spain. When the home range went forward-control, Super Beaver and Super Hippo were for export.

Following its early links with Leyland the Spanish Pegaso has established itself firmly, and acquired some export business. Pictured here is a model 1083 with drawbar trailer making its way to Madrid.

assistance of another driver, who appears to be unconcerned at the prospect of losing a day's pay, for as they say – Mañana!

Crossing the border into neighbouring Portugal it is very interesting to note a totally different trucking scene; the Spanish truck life has never had a chance of infiltrating. Portugal is much more wooded, and its roads are still intended for local donkey and ox carts – a point which is clearly seen when entering Portugal from Salamanca to Guarda over an E highway which resembles Turkey's backroads, with numerous sharp hairpins and a pot-holed width of only 3 m. This route is taken by several international long-distance trucks. In fact the only stretch of divided highway lies around Lisbon, though the main north–south arteries to Porto and Setubal are of reasonable standard too, except when leading through a village. Not surprisingly the highly over-loaded and hence under-powered trucks have much difficulty in conquering some local streets in tiny hamlets, the vehicles struggling up pot-holed alleys so steep that some even stall half-way.

Overturned trucks, even in the middle of cities, or vehicles losing part of their load are daily routine on Portuguese highways. An additional hazard is the suicidal driving style – reminiscent of Middle Eastern truckers – which prevails in Portugal, three vehicles sometimes running side-by-side downhill along a single-lane highway! A necessary status-symbol seems to be the locomotive type of air-horn or multi-tone air-horn, and these are to be found on almost every car and truck. The louder the better seems to be the name of the game and every driver is constantly trying to blast other road users off the bitumen.

Heavy articulated types of truck have appeared in Portugal only in recent years. The rigid two- and three-axle trucks still make up the greater part of fleets, and these are mostly fitted with colourful wooden or steel drop-side bodywork, and there are only a few closed van type vehicles in evidence. Due to severe overloading, the heavy tractor-trailer and drawbar combinations are exotic in appearance with a definite African flavour. Most consist of a 300+hp double-drive tandem tractor pulling a very long wheelbase heavy steel semi-trailer, generally made by Fruehauf or Titan under licence. Length limits are 15 m for an articulated vehicle and 18 m for a truck and full trailer combi-

1

nation all within a 38 tonne gcw maximum, but as is often witnessed on the road this weight limit is theoretical and most vehicles are loaded to volume capacity rather than ton capacity. A flat-bed rigid truck has been seen with such an enormous quantity of rock on its back that all four rear tyres blew out! Such novelties as hydraulic tail-lifts or cranes are seldom fitted, and with labour costs very low even tippers are often fixed-body designs carting sand and gravel, while the transport of cement in bags is a national pastime with literally hundreds of drop-side trucks queuing to get a massive load at concrete plants.

Ordinary farm tractors with small tipping trailers and geared for an amazing speed of 40 km per hour are popular on winding mountain roads for hauling sand and gravel. These machines, with rear-view mirrors and lights fitted, happily mix with the other traffic on main roads, and the driver, complete with earflaps against the screaming engine and transmission, is often seen struggling at the wheel to keep the swinging outfit on the right track. The only habit copied from the Spanish is

2

3

1. Volvo F89 with unusual part-tanker, part-general goods trailer, passing the beautiful 11th century cathedral at Batalha on the road to Porto.

2. Hauliers in Portugal are well used to having their vehicles loaded beyond the norm. This operator has chosen a rather tough looking DAF FT 2800 with double-drive axles which looks ready to hold its own.

3. The Portuguese are renowned for their stylistic coach-building, but the appearance of this locally-cabbed AEC Mammoth Major casts doubt upon their reputation.

the use heavy trucks make of the right-hand indicator to signal when it is safe for tailing motorists to overtake. This practice has gone so far in Spain itself that many trucks and buses have special small green lights fitted at the rear.

Because of the good weather, and the general lack of cash to purchase new vehicles every couple of years, many Portuguese operators keep their trucks as long as possible, hence the abundance of old battered vehicles everywhere. These are often in a really bad state of maintenance, however, except for those belonging to a handful of owner-operators running one vehicle: they seem to care more about their equipment than company drivers do. Many exquisite models of locally built Leyland, AEC, Atkinson, DAF and Scania trucks are all over Portugal, often from the early 1950s.

Leyland still produce a locally assembled truck which is unique because it sports a Scania LB 80 series cab with an Ergomatic front-styling and comes in both two- and three-axle form. Volvo is another manufacturer with Portuguese-built models and offers a forward-control chassis fitted with an odd, modified F88 cab and F86 engine and components, but designated the F85. An N7 is also built using the new sloped square bonnet but retaining the old round cab of the former N86/88. Heavier, completely imported F89 and N10/12 models plus the new F10/12 are also sold in quantity. In addition to the Mastiff, Leyland market a good number of heavy Crusaders with Detroit Diesel power, sold with the Leyland badge. But the biggest surprise on the roads in Portugal is the phenomenal number of Japanese trucks, from the tiny Daihatsu pick-ups to the massive Mitsubishi Fuso models. Portugal is the only country in Europe where all Nippon makes are successfully sold. Isuzu, Mazda and Toyota are well represented in the light- to medium-capacity categories, while Nissan, Hino and Mitsubishi are favoured for tandem-drive tractors and big rigids as well as in the lighter field.

Most other European truck manufacturers, such as DAF, Scania, MAN, Magirus-Deutz, OM, Berliet, Fiat, Unic, Saviem, Steyr, Mercedes-Benz and Pegaso are seen more or less regularly on Portuguese roads. Bedfords in both bonneted and cabover shape, including a few TM models, are very popular, as are the various Ford D-series models (but not the Transcontinentals). Another interesting vehicle often in use is the Mack MB, a forward-control model with Portuguese cab.

Despite Spain's proximity, the recent new-style Pegaso trucks are seen only occasionally, while there is no trace at all of Barreiros vehicles and very few small Ebro models have been sold so far. In fact, European manufacturers in general have to fight hard to prevent the Japanese truck forces from colouring the whole market yellow!

WEST GERMANY AND AUSTRIA

Germany has always had very advanced road networks and transport equipment, and since World War II West Germany has often led Europe in such matters. Though in the 1920s trucks all over the world looked roughly similar in layout and weights, by the 1930s Germany was setting its own standards for vehicle building and operation.

As early as 1932 a huge 150 hp Krupp-Flettner five-axle rigid truck was available with a payload of 15 tonnes! The heavy haulage tractor specialists Kaelble and Faun were also offering big highway tractors for semi-trailers up to 30 tonne capacity, while in 1936 Büssing-NAG introduced a tandem-drive conventional tractor powered by two 160 hp Otto diesel engines. This hauled a semi-trailer plus another four-axle draw-bar trailer for the transportation of 40-tonne lumberloads. (Genuine double-bottom outfits were seen not only in America.) Another popular combination in those days was the heavy Mercedes-Benz L 10.000 three-axle rigid truck pulling a three-axle drawbar trailer and with a payload capacity of over 20 tonnes, an economic proposition for their owners.

In the early 1950s heavy trucks were still the order of the day, and both multi-axle tractor-semi-trailer rigs and double-bottom outfits were seen, but in addition rigid trucks coupled to two similar drawbar trailers with a length up to 24 m plied the German Autobahns – divided concrete highways designed in the 1930s to speed up military convoys in wartime, and to be used a landing strips for the Luftwaffe's fighting planes. However, the typical heavy German rigs disappeared gradually from 1956 when the Minister of Transportation, Sebohm, introduced the most unpopular 24 tonne gross gcw regulation. Most trucks were now either rigids, light four-axle articulated or drawbar combinations within a length limit of 16.5 m.

But in the late 1950s the 32 tonne gcw limit was approved, though with an axle limit of 8 tonnes; and Mercedes introduced its twin-steer cabover LP 333 series of Chinese Six configuration with a gvw of 16 tonnes (two front-axles of 4 tonnes) capable of pulling an 8 tonne trailer before 1958 at 24 tonnes gcw, and a 16 tonne trailer for 32 tonnes gross gcw after that date. During the Sebohm period only driven axles could gross 8 tonnes, other axles only 4 tonnes, so there was a tremendous decline in revenue for heavy truck operators in West Germany and a number of the old extra-heavy

vehicles had to be scrapped. Many of the old heavy trailers were briefly reprieved in 1965, however, when the current 38 tonne gcw limit came into force, but these pre-1956 models were to prove too heavy to transport the loads at reasonable cost. But the basic single-tyred high dropside and tarpaulin-covered three-axle drawbar trailers are still the backbone of many German transport fleets. Overall length limits are now in line with most other European countries at 15 m for a tractor-semi-trailer and 18 m for a drawbar outfit, though until recently a minimum brake horse-power requirement of 8 bhp per tonne was applied, and hence most of the German manufacturers started offering V8, V10 and V12 diesel engines of around 320 bhp.

While the big engines are still retained in most chassis, the legal requirement has been reduced (in 1978) to 6 bhp per tonne, but engines of around 230 hp prove to be too light for hauling a 38 tonne gcw combination on long internal autobahn hauls where there is much undulating country to be traversed and the automobile drivers tend to keep the throttle hard down at speeds of over 160 km per hour!

Catering for weary and hungry truckers as well as tourists, many modern truck-stops, or the better rest-stops, have been erected along all major highways. Each generally has a large restaurant, bar, lounge, washing facilities for truckers, shop, service-station and small garage or tyre repair business, and these places are well patronized by drivers and motorists alike. There is always ample parking space, and while West Germany has a very large number of autobahns connecting all major cities as well as providing a fast means of crossing the entire country for long-distance traffic, thousands of heavy trucks from every corner of Europe and well beyond can be regularly seen at one of these huge rest-stops. Besides, as there is a ban on Sunday trucking – applying also to Saturdays during the summer season – hundreds of international truckers hauling non-perishable goods are forced to wait until Sunday night to

The Saurer name is synonymous with Austria. Here a D330 truck-trailer combination is seen at a dockside, waiting to be loaded.

proceed, and obviously prefer to stay at a well-equipped truck-stop than to hang around the cab for days on some deserted factory back-yard.

All international operators hauling into or through West Germany are required by law to have special permits, and for some countries only limited numbers of such transit permits are supplied, which means that the operators on long inter-Europe hauls without these permits have to detour for hundreds of miles. However, the German Federal Railways have launched their piggy-back service, hauling complete vehicles on railway wagons right across the country, and for this no permits are necessary. Of course the service is expensive. Fortunately for the international operators this kind of subsidizing of the state transport system has now ceased in West Germany and enough permits are now issued to satisfy everyone. Hauling goods under TIR coverage (Transport International Routier) means that most foreign trucks can pass the German borders without too much delay and paper-work, but all vehicles are required to report their fuel-tank contents and are required to pay tax on diesel-fuel. The consequent hold-up of approximately twenty to thirty minutes at the German border is however very quick when compared with delays on the borders of many other European countries.

Though German roads sport an enormous variety of heavy trucks, with the majority coming from abroad, home-produced commercial vehicles have rapidly dwindled during recent years, and only Mercedes-Benz, MAN and Magirus-Deutz are still on the market. Surprisingly few old Krupp, Büssing and Faun trucks are on the roads today, and almost all the heavy trucks seen are modern German products or imported Scania, Volvo, DAF, Fiat and Ford. There are a few rare Mack, OM and Saviem vehicles around, but not much else – except in the medium-weight class, where Ford, Bedford and Leyland are well represented among the home-bred products.

A world leader in heavy truck production is certainly Mercedes-Benz, who export to over 160 countries. Their commercial vehicles are of high quality, as were the L 1500, L 3000, L 4000 and L 5000 in the early 1920s, which were offered with engines up to 120 hp. In the 1930s the well-known L 2000, L 6500 and 10-tonne payload L 10.000 were developed, the latter with a 150 hp six-

1

2

1. Not the heaviest of German trucks, but medium-weight outfits like this 1950s Borgward with its six-cylinder 95-hp diesel, were widely used for inter-city work a few years ago.

2. A typical Austrian haulage outfit is this ÖAF Tornado with 256-bhp MAN diesel engine. By comparison with their German neighbours the truck products of Austria are little known in export markets.

cylinder diesel. Until 1950 Mercedes only offered normal-control chassis, which remained basically the same right up to 1961, when the still-produced round-nosed LK/LS series was launched. Cabover models thus appeared in the 1950s with engines up to 200 hp, replaced in turn by the modern angular LP series in 1963 with gcw of up to 40 tonnes, and latest models powered by V8 diesels of 320 hp and fitted with a slightly modified tilt-cab. Many of these forward-control trucks are still the backbone of German road-haulage companies, but the 1975-introduced New Generation cabover series, with engines up to 320 hp in V-10 form coupled to ZF or Fuller gearboxes, is rapidly changing the character of many European highways. With its modern aerodynamic tilt cab and excellent driver comforts plus Mercedes reliability, this particular truck has become an example for modern European heavy truck manufacturers.

MAN produced its first commercial vehicle in 1915 with an engine of 37 bhp manufactured under licence from Saurer, a practice followed by many companies at that time. After Benz, MAN was the second largest world-user of oil engines, this due to Rudolf Diesel, who used the MAN premises and vehicles for development. The company soon specialized in the heavier field, having a 10-tonner three-axle truck of 150 hp on offer in 1927. After World War II the conventional MAN MK series became popular around the world and was even offered with the world's first V-8 diesel of 150 hp in 1950. MAN took over the Büssing plant in 1971 and gradually built their own cabs around the famous Büssing underfloor-engined chassis, which are still marketed. MAN also have an arrangement with Saviem in France, each sharing the other's components. There is a similar arrangement with ÖAF and Gräf & Stift in Austria. The heavier MAN vehicles are powered by Mercedes-Benz V engines. In 1979 the new Volkswagen-MAN medium-capacity truck will be launched, a small cabover jointly developed and giving MAN more ability to compete in the lower weight classes.

Magirus originally built fire engines, but introduced the first trucks around 1916. The diesel engines appeared in 1932 and were soon up to twelve-cylinder 150 hp units. Magirus joined with Deutz in 1935, and vehicles were afterwards optionally fitted with air-cooled diesels, still the standard feature of all Magirus-Deutz trucks.

After World War II the famous round-nosed conventional was introduced as well as cabovers with air-cooled diesels with up to 200 hp, and these types were superseded by new models in the early 1960s with increased engine power. In 1971 the current conventional angular normal-control chassis was introduced, and the vehicles have found ready acceptance in on- and off-highway construction work, while the modern cabovers with the latest Fiat tilt cab are intended for long distance haulage and powered by V8 or V10 diesels of up to 340 hp, of course air-cooled. Magirus is part of the huge Iveco Group with Fiat, Lancia, OM, and Unic, and many parts including engines and cabs are common. The company also developed jointly with DAF, Saviem and Volvo the Club of Four medium-capacity forward-control vehicles.

Büssing built their first commercial vehicle in 1903, offering heavy tandem-axle trucks of normal-control construction and which by 1924 were powered by 120 hp Maybach engines. Following co-operation with NAG, the first diesel-engined chassis in the conventional Burglöwe was produced from 1932 onwards, but after the war this became a cabover model. After 1945 production centred around the long-nosed conventional types, but a revolutionary underfloor-engined forward-control truck designated the U 12000 with 175 hp six-cylinder diesel and separately driven tandem rear-axles was launched in 1951 and was typical of the heavy long-distance trucks in Germany at the time. The last series of cabover models introduced before the take-over in 1971 by MAN consisted of both underfloor and normal engined tilt cab tractors and trucks with power up to 320 hp. These vehicles were praised by drivers for their silence and comfortable ride, while mechanics liked the accessibility to maintenance of the underfloor engines. This was why MAN continued to offer the basic chassis of Büssing, though with a MAN tilt cab. Many of the more recent genuine Büssings can still be seen operating all over West Germany and in many countries abroad, and it is a shame that such a reputable and long-established firm could not remain independent.

The same applies to Henschel, a company which started building Swiss FBW trucks under licence in 1925 but later developed their own chassis, offering already in the 1930s models from 60 to 250 hp with either petrol or diesel engines of up to twelve cylin-

ders. Post-World War II models included both normal- and forward-control chassis, all with diesel-engines and either 4×2, 4×4, 6×4 or 6×6 drive, and many of the conventional models were exported to other European countries and to Africa, where many can be found still working after twenty-five years or more. In 1960 a completely new Henschel range appeared in both normal and cabover form with very modern angular cabs, later labelled Hanomag-Henschels after the merger in 1968 with Rheinstahl-Hanomag. The range remained in production, though updated, until the take-over by the Daimler-Benz concern. Hanomag was well-known in the 1930–45 period for road-tractors with gtw (gross train weights) of up to 20 tonnes and capable of high speeds. The firm also tried producing an underfloor-engined type in 1936 and various normal-control models, but after World War II concentrated on light- to medium-capacity vehicles.

The name Krupp has been almost synonymous with Germany for very many years. The firm entered the vehicle-building industry in 1920 and manufactured both forward- and normal-control

Greek truckers on an international haul pause at an alpine roadhouse. The Austrian Alps are crossed by an almost endless string of trucks going about their everyday business, much to the annoyance of many Austrians.

models of up to 75 hp during the 1930s. Later they experimented with the two-stroke Junker engine, which resulted in four-, six-, and eight-cylinder engines plus a four-cylinder air-cooled design. In common with other German truck manufacturers, Krupp experienced considerable losses through World War II, and no new models were announced until the early 1950s. These were diesels of up to 160 hp – and even a 200 hp five-cylinder two-stroke some years later – which were eventually replaced by four-stroke Cummins diesels in 1964 with bhp ratings of 250 and 265 for the V8. Krupp built several normal- and forward-control models during its last years, before production ceased completely in 1968, but many old Krupps are seen on the road, particularly outside Germany.

Few manufacturers have survived in the truck field although many were long established in

Germany and had sales abroad. One survivor is Kaelble who specialized early in developing heavy haulage tractors, and in 1933 made some tractors for 100 tonne-plus loads of railway wagons, complete with multi-axle trailers. These were followed in 1937 by another design for the Federal Railways, this time an all-wheel-drive cabover tractor with 200 hp diesel amidships mounted in reverse, and with both the front axle and the rearmost axle of the tandem steering. Kaelble also produced a series of on-highway trucks with normal- or forward-control cabs in the late 1940s and early 1950s, but after that period production concentrated again on heavy haulage prime movers, and today three- and four-axle all-wheel drive vehicles with Mercedes diesels of up to 880 hp and gtw of 1,000 tonnes are marketed alongside industrial tractors, dumpers and construction machinery.

Faun has a similar story, commencing in 1928 using Deutz air-cooled engines and always specializing in unusual heavy tractors and trucks, such as the cabover eight-wheelers of the mid-1930s and wartime heavy tank transporters. In addition Faun established itself as a well-known manufacturer of fire-engines, crane-carriers and municipal vehicles over the years, built a number of conventional and cabover highway models in the 1950s and introduced a new tilt cab highway tractor and truck in 1967 powered by Deutz 250 or 300 hp V-10 diesels. Only a limited number of these were built and they are seldom seen today. Faun now offers a whole range of heavy haulage tractors with two, three or four axles, mostly of conventional design with or without all-wheel drive, and with diesel engines up to 860 hp. Not surprisingly these well engineered German giants found their way all over the world to perform the mighty task of pulling huge indivisible loads. In West Germany itself big heavy haulage jobs are mostly carried out during the night to avoid inconvenience to traffic and the giants are seldom seen by the public. Much heavy equipment is transported on wheels only as far as a nearby quay, where it is loaded on a barge for further transportation through one of the many waterways.

German trucks are not generally considered Europe's smartest, for most vehicles come in ordinary colours without frills, and weird axle-combinations or body-setups are not allowed. German truck drivers are distinguished by their high salary, and it is not unusual for a long-distance trucker to earn the same as a doctor and to come to work in a big Mercedes or BMW saloon!

Looking across the southern border we encounter the Austrian truckers who might not earn so much cash but do have an interest in the appearance of their vehicles. It is quite difficult to keep a truck in fine fettle, however, in the long cold winter with lots of salt and mud on the heavy truck roads leading through the Alps. The main highway leading towards the Balkans and beyond is laid from West to East through Austria's lower valleys, and consists to a great extent of narrow twisting single-lane highway, with a cosy *Gasthaus* or two along the way for the tired trucker to get a shower or a good meal. These old-style rest- or road-houses are not modern, but are clean and hospitable and on the whole reasonably priced (except for the coffee). There are very few big restaurants with all the facilities for the car or truck driver, and those that there are tend to be situated along stretches of divided highway near Salzburg and in the south. The majority of roads are of the wide two-lane type with a third lane for heavy trucks on hills, and often these roads follow the bank of a river through valleys and picturesque villages with small alleys of cobbled stone which are obviously not suitable for heavy long-distance trucks. In winter the snow is often blown across the roads by the strong valley winds, but it is instantly cleared by efficient snow-ploughs working by day or night, while road gangs clean up the markers and direction signs as well. Though no snow-chains are needed on a cross-country Austrian haul many trucks do still carry these for when they run into a bad snowstorm or when the destination is high up a mountain-pass.

Austria is spending a lot of money on opening up new road networks, a prime example being the recently opened Arlberg tunnel, at 14 km the longest road-tunnel in the world, and built in only fifty-three months. The high cost of such projects and the fact that foreign vehicles make extensive use of Austrian international routes brought the government to enforce the ill-received transit tax. This objectionable legislation was highlighted in 1978 by a big blockade of border crossings by thousands of international and Austrian truckers who protested by effectively closing every road for days on end.

Many other countries retaliated against these

very confusing new regulations by requiring that Austrian international operators should pay taxes when outside their country. So now the Austrian government has to use the transit dues to support their own haulage companies. Regarding the enforcement of other regulations, the police are not very much in evidence on Austrian roads, and weighbridges are rare. Most truckers do keep to the 80 km per hour limit, however, and generally do not overload their vehicles.

The enormous amount of international traffic using the main highway from the German–Austrian border near Salzburg to the crossing with Yugoslavia near Graz can be gauged from the fact that even TR, YU and GR decals, denoting Turkey, Yugoslavia and Greece, have been added to road-signs in Austria to guide these trucks on their way. Thousands of foreign trucks move daily in convoy, tailing each other because it is difficult to overtake on the twisting black ribbon.

The Austrians themselves mix happily with this international bunch, but though there are a good number of Mercedes, MAN, Magirus, Volvo, Scania and DAF trucks, operators are very patriotic to judge by the great number of Steyr Plus series trucks around, while ÖAF and Gräf & Stift, plus the Austrian Saurer make up the rest of the scene.

Steyr built only cars at first, but their truck production commenced in 1927, and several light models were manufactured until the company formed Steyr-Daimler-Puch AG, when new types were developed with emphasis on four-wheel drive vehicles. These became famous for their strength and robustness, as did the entire truck range. It was not until 1947 that the first Steyr diesel was produced and fitted to the 380, 480 and 580 trucks of the early 1950s, followed in the 1960s by the heavier types 586, 680 and 780 in both normal- and forward-control models. At the end of 1968 the present Plus series was announced, and these very modern tilt-cab tractors and trucks with diesel engines up to 400 hp in V12 form driving through ZF nine- or twelve-speed gearboxes come in various configurations, including 6×6 all-wheel drive, eight-wheeler rigid or twin-steer tractor with detractable pusher-steering axle. Steyr export to many countries around the world and the firm is a true example of quality engineered heavy truck manufacturing.

ÖAF started building commercial vehicles

1

2

1. *Typical of German logging operations is this MAN 10126 HSA tractor coupled to Doll widespread tandem logging bogie.*

2. *Mercedes-Benz 'New Generation' 2232 model with 320 hp engine. The introduction of this new series of trucks heralded renewed pressure on export markets by German truck-builders.*

3. *Once a common sight on German and Austrian roads were Henschel outfits similar to this.*

4. *Dating from the 1960s is this smart Austrian-built Gräf & Stift L230 with Mercedes-Benz engine.*

under the brand-name AF (Austro-Fiat), working under licence from Fiat, but later MAN components were used and then complete MAN trucks assembled for the Austrian market. In the early 1950s ÖAF designed their own trucks which used either their own engines or those of MAN, Leyland or Cummins, and typical types of 1960 were the Tornado normal-control trucks, of which many can still be seen on the Austrian roads. In the 1960s, too, new cabovers with very smart clean

3

4

bodywork were launched, together with short-nosed conventionals in the 980 series, of which many were exported to Spain and are still used extensively. Recent ÖAF vehicles are more to MAN design again and are fitted with MAN diesel engines of up to 320 hp in the on- and off-highway Jumbo series.

Gräf & Stift has now merged with ÖAF, but produced their first commercial vehicles in 1919, and over the years almost all components were home-produced and developed. In 1958 new trucks were built offering Mercedes-Benz diesels of up to 200 hp, which were built during the 1960s under licence and fitted to both conventionals and cabover trucks; only a few survive today.

The last Austrian maker is Saurer, initially an off-shoot of the Swiss company, but later manufacturing completely self-developed vehicles with petrol or diesel engines until World War II. After wartime production of military vehicles new trucks were announced, mainly of normal-control lay-out with engines of up to 180 hp and eight cylinders. Cabover models were added in 1958, though not for long because a few years later Saurer joined Steyr-Daimler-Puch and production was slowly discontinued. The same problem applies all over the world: the big companies submerge the smaller independents and many distinguished models and makes are doomed to disappear. Fortunately Austrian operators are often small independent businesses with pride in the bygone products, and a fair number of old but well built ÖAF, Saurer and Gräf & Stift models still rumble around the Alps.

SWITZERLAND AND ITALY

The beautiful mountain scenery of Switzerland may be an ideal place for the tourist to relax, but for the local truck operators it means work of a much more demanding nature than is found in countries with flat land. Switzerland is considered a rich country, and many francs have been spent on constructing multi-lane highways between the major cities, including often ingenious constructions and fly-overs to bypass city centres or difficult mountain valleys. However, there are still many miles of narrow winding mountain roads with passes at almost 3,000 m. Several tunnels for both road and rail transport have been cut through the Alps, the longest being the Simplon tunnel between Switzerland and Italy, measuring almost 20 m in length. Obviously many of the mountain passes are closed during winter, which can last from early October until May due to severe snowfall. Swiss road maintenance authorities try to keep as many roads as possible open all year round, but even with all-wheel drive and snowchains trucking in wintery Switzerland is just not possible in some areas. To avoid time-consuming driving over high Alpine passes many trucks make use of the railways' Hukepack system: vehicles are loaded on trains and carried through the tunnels. Though quite expensive this method is always better than driving uphill and downhill in an endless queue of tourist cars in mid-summer or through walls of snow piled several metres high in winter – if the pass is open for traffic at all. Snow-chains are compulsory on many roads.

Because many roads are actually unsuitable for heavy traffic the Swiss government has enacted a law of 2.30 m maximum width and a maximum total weight of 28 tonnes for all combinations. However, these limits only apply to vehicles operated on domestic haulage, and Swiss operators of long-distance trucks can get permission to use 38 tonne normal international TIR type combinations from within certain points of Switzerland to the nearest border. Despite the difficult mountain driving a lot of tractor-semi-trailer or drawbar outfits are in operation, but the widespread single-tyred axles of 12 m semi-trailers are usually of the self-steering type to negotiate tight curves.

For local haulage the heavy single-axle trailer behind a rigid truck is popular here as in Sweden, and is clearly a useful combination at higher altitudes. However, recent developments show a

1
2

1. To any truck buff visiting Switzerland the sight of one of the American Kenworths, imported direct from the USA by Friderici of Morges, is a true delight.

2. This modern 5DF 6×4 Saurer is used by an enterprising Swiss haulier for the gruelling Middle East trip. He prefers the home-grown trucks to the more prolific Swedish and German imports.

3. Swiss trucks always look well cared for, and this old Diamond T is certainly a case in point.

tendency to operate more and more heavy four-axle rigid trucks, most of them similar to the British eight-wheeler with twin-steer front axles and double-drive bogie. There are also many conversions of basically tandem-drive three-axle long wheel-base chassis with a fourth steering (single-tyred) axle in front or behind the rear bogie. These big rigids can gross 28 tonnes, which is the same maximum as for a semi- or full trailer combination, but manoeuvrability is greatly improved. Many manufacturers offer such eight-wheelers now, but Saurer/Berna clearly leads the line with the D 330 or 5 DF type.

The first Saurer trucks of 1903 set the pace for a whole range of commercial vehicles built all over Europe and in the United States under licence. Saurer was also the first builder of a diesel engine way back in 1908. After producing A and B ranges with diesels of up to 40 hp in both tractor and truck chassis, the C range was introduced in 1933, featuring up to 9.5 tons payload in both normal- and forward-control form and also built by Berna. These models were produced until 1960. During World War II many all-wheel-drive military vehicles were produced, and are still manufactured in limited numbers, but the conventional and cabover highway models in the 4 and 5 D, DU, DM and DF, together with the D 330 series make up the greater part of production today. The heaviest types are powered by a 330 hp diesel coupled to a nine-speed ZF gearbox or Allison Automatic and capable of hauling up to 100 tonne gross loads. Many of the latter types are also marketed under the Berna badge. This company worked together with Saurer from 1929 and the complete merger took place in 1939, when the Berna line of trucks in the medium-weight capacity was replaced by Saurer models of the C series (but sold as Berna U types). OM light trucks and vans are manufactured under licence for the local Swiss market. Saurer/Berna is Switzerland's main truck manufacturer, and builds a whole range of passenger buses and stationary engines as well, with a good export reputation for all products recently.

The next Swiss company to consider is that of Franz Brozincevic of Wetzikon, better known as the producer of FBW trucks and buses dating back to 1911, when they launched their first 5-ton truck with cardan-drive, a European novelty. The products of FBW were famous for their reliability and sturdiness, which was why the German Henschel company started building trucks of FBW design before engaging in development themselves. Having built a whole range of chassis over the years for both tipper, general goods and municipal needs the company is still known for its quality engineering instead of mass-production. No wonder many old FBW conventional and cabover trucks are still earning money for their owners all over Switzerland today. Underfloor-engined vehicles have been an FBW speciality since 1949 and current production includes several two-, three- and even four-axle chassis with underfloor diesels up to 320 hp and twelve-speed ZF gearbox or Allison Automatic. Both conventional and cabover models with very modern styling are offered. Another manufacturer primarily of light- and medium-capacity vehicles is Mowag, who now specialize in all-wheel-drive trucks, but build a number of cabovers, more as prototypes, as well, including a huge cabover eight-wheel twin-steer rigid with the Mowag underfloor diesel of 500 hp.

Alusuisse is a well-known Swiss manufacturer of all-aluminium bodywork for trucks, trailers and buses around the world, but the firm only recently ventured into the field of developing their own truck, a cabover rigid chassis of aluminium construction saving several hundred pounds of weight over a comparable steel-based vehicle. The bright attractive appearance of many trucks in Switzerland is because of fitted aluminium superstructures, generous painting in lively colours, and the conscientious attitude of the truckers themselves, who really care about their equipment.

Though Swiss operators favour national products, many foreign trucks are imported, with Volvo, Scania, Mercedes-Benz, Fiat, Magirus-Deutz, MAN, Steyr and DAF all selling in quantity on a total market of approximately 120,000 units a year. But there are a great many more types of foreign trucks regularly plying the Swiss or international roads, among which are numbered the ERF B-series and 'European', old Seddons and many Leyland models, Ford Transcontinentals, a few Bedford TMs with the popular TK and KM series, Dodge Commandos, Japanese Hinos and Mitsubishi Fuso's, plus the French makes of Saviem, Unic and Berliet. Most impressive of all are the big American Macks, White and even Kenworth trucks. Kenworth have a distributor in

Zurich offering both conventional and cabover models, including the big Transorient (modified Aerodyne in the United States) with double bunks and all kitchen utensils for extra-long-distance operations. In fact the Swiss company of Friderici in Morges near the Lake of Geneva is the biggest European Kenworth operator with over 40 cabover two- and three-axle tractors and trucks on international haulage as far away as Saudi Arabia. The vehicles are directly imported from the United States and sport aluminium chassis and tanks, with 430 hp Detroit Diesels and Fuller thirteen-speed gearboxes in the heaviest types, which also have modified aluminium air-intake stacks behind the cab to accommodate longer bodywork on the rigids. Front axles, which are set back, are also specified by Friderici. This haulage company is noted for Swiss efficiency and cleanliness in its ultra-modern workshop and warehouses, while pride in work and equipment is reflected in the company's drivers, who always take out the same vehicle.

To supply the operators with the best possible local truck needs several foreign manufacturers have specially modified 230 cm width vehicles on sale, such as the DAF 2800 for Switzerland, which is a narrower heavy-duty chassis from the 2800 series with a slightly different 2300 series cab. In addition to DAF, Scania, Volvo, OM, Steyr and Magirus-Deutz all offer eight-wheel rigids of 230 cm width for the maximum 28 tonne gross allowed. Right-hand drive is often fitted, though predominantly on older vehicles and trucks used on Alpine roads, this arrangement giving far better sight on the nearside edge of the ravine or rockface and enabling the driver to steer his rig as precisely as possible.

Because Italy borders on Switzerland in the south and almost everything in the southern Swiss Alp regions is completely Italian orientated many trucks tend to show similarities with the vehicles operated in Italy, meaning not only the right-hand steering wheel arrangement but the overall design as well – such as the addition of trailing axles on both rigid trucks and trailers. The Italian influence is also noted in the choice of vehicles: a lot more OM, Fiat and Lancia models in all weight categories are used by operators in the south than by those from north of the Alps in Switzerland.

In 1976 the Italians moved their maximum

1

2

3

1. Danzas operate this impressive Saurer 5DF 8×4 of 330 hp, legally operating at 28 tonnes gross.

2. Better known for their cars, the Alfa-Romeo marque once boasted a fine range of trucks.

3. Typical modern Italian practice is portrayed by this 170NT Fiat tractor unit coupled to a skeletal semi with unusual axle spacing and a self-steering rearmost axle.

weight limits drastically upwards from 32 tonnes to 44 tonnes gross for a tractor-semi-trailer or truck-trailer combination with five or more axles, a change made without any consultation with the EEC countries, who have argued about new limits for years. Though not the highest gcw in Europe the increase of 12 tonnes for the heaviest vehicle must certainly help the productivity of Italian haulage companies.

Following the rapid increase in normal two-axle tractor coupled to three-axle semi-trailer combinations seen on Italian roads recently, after the new liberal weight limits, the practice of overloading vehicles has been eliminated completely. Previously permitted axle-weights were 10 tonnes for a single and 14.5 tonnes for a bogie set-up, and consequently typical Italian maximum-gross vehicles consisted of a four-axle rigid hauling a three- or four-axle full trailer with many of the axles being of the single-tyred trailing type. Though these outfits are still operated they will certainly fade away as time goes on. Overall length for a drawbar outfit is 18 m, and for a tractor-semi-trailer rig 15.5 m.

At the same time, however, the Italian government insisted on an increase of power for the various commercial vehicles, and the requirement is 8 bhp/ton gvw, which means that at least 352 bhp is needed to propel the 44 tonne gcw rigs, giving them ample power to keep pace with normal traffic under most road conditions. Italy has built a very modern and efficient highway network over the last ten years, and though these levy high tolls on commercial vehicles most operators prefer to use these (contrary to the French practice) instead of the small overcrowded country roads which are totally unsuited to heavy traffic, with numerous villages to negotiate and all sorts of road-users from the past, such as horses and donkey-carts. As in most Western European countries hauliers on international TIR work use tilt tarpaulin-covered vehicles extensively, while the Italians are also well known for their beautiful clean-looking refrigerated van-bodied combinations hauling meat and fruit all over Europe. But in Italy itself pressed-steel dropside bodywork is most favoured for general haulage operations.

Italy is associated with sun and automobiles, and Fiat takes the lion's share in many fields, including commercial vehicles. Almost half the registrations on the roads come from this huge concern, which

1

2

formed part of the IVECO (Industrial Vehicles Corporation) Group with Magirus-Deutz of Germany, Unic in France, and OM and Lancia in Italy to develop and market vehicles jointly around the world. Certainly Fiat has a long reputation: the first truck was produced in 1903, a 24 hp 4-tonner.

After World War II Fiat concentrated further on forward-control models, although the C40, a bonneted version, was built until 1959, and both power and weights have increased over the years up to the present 170 series cabover tractors and trucks.

1. *Although retaining an individual badge and marketing organization, OM has been part of the Fiat group since 1938, hence the cab similarity. Here an OM 190 model takes on a load of Italian marble.*

2. *For many years Fiat have produced a rigid eight-wheel chassis, and often these could be found with long eight-wheel trailers, having odd axle spacing to circumvent restrictive axle-loading regulations.*

These come with the new IVECO tilt cab also fitted with minor modifications to Magirus and Unic vehicles and are powered by the six-cylinder 260 hp or V8 356 hp diesel coupled to Fuller nine- or thirteen-speed transmissions. Fiat offers a whole range of cabover vehicles from vans and 4×4 off-highway trucks to buses and sleeper-cab long-distance tractors, and these find their way to many operators in Europe, Africa, Asia and Australia. Fiat's partner OM started truck production in 1930 with a light-vehicle range based on their earlier

cars, and soon they were offering heavier vehicles under a licence agreement with Swiss Saurer, top of the range being the Super Orione with a 170 hp V8 diesel engine manufactured in the early 1950s.

IVECO's third Italian member is Lancia, whose involvement in truck-building stems from 1915 when the company offered many chassis for both military and civilian purposes, generally of normal-control layout. In 1950 the then bonneted Esatau range was reshaped into a forward-control model powered with a 132-hp diesel. This was followed in 1959 and 1962 by the Esadelta and Esagamma ranges respectively, and Lancia progressed in the higher horsepower field with engines of up to 240 hp and 275 hp and with very modern forward-control cabs. Many of these vehicles still operate on the Italian highways of today. Lancia now concentrate on light commercials and special-purpose vehicles in the IVECO group.

Alfa-Romeo no longer rank among the Italian heavy-duty truck manufacturers. They once produced a distinct line of commercial vehicles with very artistic forward-control cabs and engines of Büssing origin. Tipo 50, with an 80-hp diesel for a 5-ton payload, was the first model in 1930, and Tipo 350 followed in the late 1930s. After World War II new trucks were launched in the 9000 series with 130-hp engines, and these were superseded in turn by the Mille two- and three-axle tractors and trucks with up to 175 hp diesels in the late 1950s and early 1960s, which are still built in Brazil under licence by FNM. Production at Alfa-Romeo in Italy is now centred solely around light Saviem-type commercials and cars.

Since Italy became a member of the EEC Italian truck operators have had a much wider choice of commercial vehicles, and several Scania, Volvo and Ford Transcontinental trucks have found their way south, most of these vehicles with the highest engine option available in the 350 hp and over category, to enable hauling of 44-tonne trains. Ford with its E 390 in the Transcontinental range and Berliet with the TR 350 are hoping to sell several chassis in the top weight class on the Italian market. DAF, Unic, Bedford, MAN and of course Magirus (as another IVECO member) all try to get a hold on the market in Italy, where almost 70 per cent of goods carried go by road, and all these makes will add a bit more colour to the now frequent sight of uniform tractor-semi-trailer rigs.

EASTERN EUROPE

One of the most intriguing areas of trucking is that of the Eastern European states for, although they embrace some of the oldest kingdoms, their truck production has not progressed at the same rate as elsewhere. This state of affairs could well change in the near future.

The old and the new transport waggons meet in Greece.

GREECE

The Greek population of nine million, in common with those of many other countries, relies heavily on road transport to get goods moved within their boundaries as well as across an ever-increasing international market. There are no waterways, and the railways are used mainly for the transportation of a few bulk commodities, and passengers in a very limited area. Trucking on mainland Greece is not a great challenge because well-laid modern highways, most of them wide and single-lane, connect major cities, and there are no really severe mountains to negotiate. The biggest delays for road traffic are experienced at the numerous inter-island ferries which keep almost two million inhabitants of the various islands in touch with the mainland. Many of these ferries are too small for the larger number of heavy vehicles making the crossing, and so long hours of waiting are unavoidable. Fortunately time is less critical than it is in more Western parts of Europe.

Although the roads are generally of a good standard the excessive mid-summer temperatures play havoc with tyres, and hundreds of blown-out truck tyres litter the shoulders of main arteries. As in other southern countries ox-, donkey- or horse-power is still used throughout Greece and these unlit and very slow road-users make driving at night very dangerous. In startling contrast to these age-old transport methods modern Greek trucks are lit in true Middle Eastern style with green, yellow, blue, amber and red marker-lights all around – a feast of colour roaring in the dark.

Because many heavy trucks have to slow down or stop at unsuitable places along the roads owing to break-downs or unloading, many sport a hazard light on the cab roof, which can often be seen fitted to long-distance international rigs. Another typically 'African' item is the fitting of a speaker on top to advertise the merchandise carried when supplying local markets. In addition many Greek truckers proudly advertise the name of the truck or some other manufacturer on the trailer sides. For example, one may see DAF, Hino or Thermo King advertised in broad lettering. Whether the respective drivers or companies receive sponsorship for this is not known.

The majority of road vehicles consist of rigid two- and three-axle trucks often with very colourful wooden body-work or clean aluminium tank- or van-bodies fitted. For long-distance haul-age within Greece tractor-semi-trailer rigs are the thing, but with many a Greek operator driving towards Western Europe and into the Middle East a lot of TIR-type tilt drawbar outfits are in operation, as well as several beautifully built white refrigerated van semi-trailers. Most loads consist of subtropical fruits for major European cities, and return-loads of anything from machinery to electrical equipment. Although length limits for articulated vehicles are 18 m these long vehicles are never seen, perhaps because they are difficult to manoeuvre on winding roads. The maximum permitted for a truck and full trailer combination is also 18 m, while 35 tonnes gross is the limit for both. In addition a small number of Spanish-type eight-wheelers are used, i.e. a rigid twin-steer with drive-axle and steerable tag-axle at the rear, and there are also a few big rigids with a tri-axle bogie manufactured by Mack in particular. These vehicles come in at 26 tonnes gvw. While regulation of truck traffic is not as stringent as in Europe or America, truck weigh-scales are set up along a number of main highways. Overloading is not therefore as bad a problem as in African or Asian countries. Though trucking is not permitted on Sundays and holidays between the hours of 07.00 and 23.00, there are still a great number of commercials on the roads on these days because of the highly perishable cargoes they carry.

There are no big truck-stops in Greece; instead many cosy small cafés are to be enjoyed with a shaded terrace where the weary trucker can have a cheap cold drink or a simple meal after dodging herds of goats or sight-seeing Western tourists.

Air-conditioning in truck cabs would be a great boon in the 40°C. temperatures and upwards, but these luxury items are probably too expensive for the Greeks, so many a trucker removes his grille to improve airflow around the engine and inside the cab. Bonneted trucks can be seen too with the hood fastened open. The fact that there are still many old vehicles around proves that maintenance is carried out properly. Clearly the problems of vehicles rusting are less acute in warm climates. Most trucks are

By the time one reaches Greece the mystic ancient Ottoman influence is just over the horizon. This Greek owner-operator has exercised his considerable skills to make his truck a showpiece.

2

1

3

not only kept clean on the outside but are also lavishly decorated inside with curtains, pictures and mascots – and a row of orchestrated airhorns are a must for any self-respecting Greek trucker. About 1,200 new heavy trucks are registered annually and these include a wide variety of models from all kinds of manufacturers.

Greece itself has no commercial vehicle producers, except for the Austrian Steyr Plus series trucks and tractors built under licence since 1972. Almost all the European makes are imported, the majority being Volvo N86-88 and F88 plus the newer N-series, Scania 110, both conventional and cabover, Mercedes-Benz older cabovers and bonneted models. Many of the 1960s long-nosed Mercedes types L312, L322 and L334 can still be seen, with old Bussing Commodores and newer underfloor-engined types often used on international hauls. Berliet, MAN, DAF, OM, Fiat and Leyland trucks, old and new, share the roads with several Japanese imports such as the Hino HE, Nissan CW 40/50 and Toyota conventional, plus a mixture of Eastern bloc types such as the Raba,

1. A Greek-registered TIR Volvo and trailer outfit sits patiently on the quayside at Rotterdam awaiting a boat.

2. Macks are popular in Greece, and this refrigerated outfit is used on the Europe–Middle East route.

3. A very rare beast is this rigid eight-wheel Volvo F88 with steering trailing axle, which can operate at 30 tonnes gross within Greek legislation.

Star and the Russian Maz.

The Seddon Atkinson 400 series is spotted regularly, as well as Foden RC types in eight-wheeler form. Finally come a whole line of American heavies such as F-model Macks, Kenworth K-123 cabovers and White Road Commanders. The majority of makes in the lower weight classes are Bedford, Mercedes, Russian Zuk and Spanish Ebro, plus almost all the light Japanese pick-up trucks. All-in-all quite a diversified trucking fraternity in sunny Greece.

THE EASTERN BLOC

Though many people now spend their annual holidays on the sunny coasts of the Adriatic and Black Sea, probably very few notice the different style of road transport in the Balkan countries and the differences in equipment. The presence of all sorts of trucks is, however, obvious, and the Communist economy depends on them heavily. Railways are of limited importance and not really up to date: steam traction is still used extensively in Hungary, Romania, Bulgaria and Yugoslavia.

Although most roads are of bitumen they are often circuitous and seldom level, rendering some parts extremely dangerous, particularly the mountainous coastal highways. Hundreds of wrecked cars and trucks can be seen on cliff-tops and in canyons along the Adriatic coast of Yugoslavia. Guard-rails are seldom fitted on bends because the road maintenance crews are unable to replace them before another vehicle demolishes them again. Although the famous Balkan truck-route, the Autoput, which runs from the Austrian border through Yugoslavia and Bulgaria into Turkey, is not as twisting as a mountain road, it is equally dangerous and is far removed from a modern Western divided highway. For the greater part of its length it is a single-lane highway punctuated by numerous railway level crossings and constantly curving or undulating.

Reckless driving is common, as road-users, including many international truckers, fight each other for precedence. Yugoslavs themselves create most of the fun – imagine a luxury coach and two heavy trucks racing side by side down a 6 m road. No wonder that almost every mile a totally demolished car or overturned truck is encountered on either side of the road. To describe a few specific mishaps: a five-axle 'semi' on a mountain section left the road and fell down a 200 m slope to land upturned and unloaded, spilling its entire cargo of boxes and crates all around and down into a river. A TAM reefer truck had a fight with a tourist coach, tearing off the whole rear end and leaving several of the back-seat passengers in the open air; both vehicles then ran off the road. Still in Yugoslavia, a drawbar bitumen tanker collided head-on with another truck, the trailer of the tanker outfit lying in a ditch half-a-mile away and the remains of the other vehicles burned out underneath an overpass. There is no sweet trucking in the Balkans! Even whole families packed in tiny Zastavas and Trabants seem to think they are invulnerable and cannot resist the temptation to find out who is the stronger – the 30-tonner or themselves.

Many accidents or near-accidents occur when high-powered Western rigs try to leapfrog the slower local trucks which trundle along at a steady 40 mph. If there is a slight incline this means that impatient truckers must put up with five or ten miles at a snail's pace. Two other possible hazards – herds of animals on the road or unlit vehicles at night – are not frequent occurrences but nor are they exceptional.

There are a considerable number of imported European trucks in Bulgaria, Romania, Hungary, Czechoslovakia and Yugoslavia, but it is the predominance of the old Eastern-bloc vehicles which reduces traffic speed. Most of these ageing trucks are under-powered diesels with gearboxes of only five or six speeds fitted to dated Skoda, Jelcz, Csepel, Maz, Belaz, Ikarus, IFA and Raba or Yugoslav TAM and FAP trucks. The newer models, like the Skoda Liaz, Tatra, Roman and Raba with 200-hp-plus engines and ten-speed boxes make life for an underpaid Balkan trucker more enjoyable, though colleagues or comrades with fancy Volvo F12, Scania 140 or Mercedes 1932 models are still looked upon as big lottery winners.

The TAM, produced in Maribor, Slovania, under licence from the German Magirus-Deutz company, is offered with air-cooled engines up to 125 hp and a gcw of 17 tonnes – obviously giving no spectacular acceleration or speed when towing a trailer, as they still frequently do. The other Yugoslav truck manufacturer, FAP, is now building modified 'New Generation' Mercedes trucks in the middle-weight class alongside its own Model 15 cabover series, trucks resembling the old Henschel cabovers. The older cabovers and the still-produced conventional 13 series truck and tractor are in fact Saurer designs and are seen in many countries of the Eastern bloc. Power for the heaviest FAP cabovers comes from a six-cylinder 200-hp diesel coupled to a six-speed gearbox, some with a two-speed rear axle. But their output figures are still rather inadequate for pulling a 40 tonne gcw drawbar outfit over mountainous terrain, and accordingly the drivers are not too enthusiastic about them.

Leyland is the only British manufacturer on view, and it is not represented in great numbers or

by the latest models. Bedford CF vans do quite well along with Ford Transits – in competition with vans by Mercedes, Fiat, Zastava, TAM and Russian Zuk. Indian-produced Tata cabover rigids fitted with Mercedes running gear and used in the middle-weight classes are a rare sight. On the heavier side foreign imports in Yugoslavia include an enormous number of OM Titano trucks still plying the highways and byways, and even a few F-model Macks.

Many combinations follow the Italian style, using trailing axles on both truck and trailer, the latter being almost invariably of Yugoslav Itas or Gorika manufacture. As in other Alpine countries trucks in the Balkans often feature right-hand drive, especially the older models.

Because most truck operations are state-controlled and owned there are no signs of scales or weighing stations, but a few police checkpoints are set up along major routes to keep an eye on the progress of state-owned equipment – which invariably appears in drab green, grey, blue or red colours, like the Czechoslovakian Skoda vehicles often seen. Neither does there seem to be any sort

The Skoda works in Czechoslovakia has been producing trucks since 1924 and once built steam lorries under licence from Sentinel. This early post-war model was operated from Romania when photographed in West Germany.

of regulation aimed at controlling air pollution by diesel trucks, though this would perhaps not be a feasible objective with the low-grade fuel available in that part of the world. Many trucks feature a kind of 'open exhaust' system which gives a hollow ear-knocking rumble reminiscent of the Spanish Pegaso. Even on Sundays many vehicles can be seen hauling all kinds of goods and carrying out their daily duties. However, there are some roads which are closed to heavy commercials on Fridays and Sundays from 3 pm until 8 or 10 pm all year round, and the ban also applies to summer Saturdays. Long queues of trucks can then be seen waiting by the roadside, their drivers taking a nap underneath the trailer to escape the summer heat.

Unlike their Western European counterparts the majority of Eastern bloc truckers have to be content with little luxury in their often old-fashioned cabs with hardly any ventilation. Except for the small windows, radiator filler-caps and scuttle ventilators they are devoid of assisted air flows, and some drivers fit a small fan behind the scuttle to help keep cool. It is no wonder many drivers on the coastal highways regularly park their rigs near the beach and take a cool swim in the deep blue water, though some tend to exaggerate by taking the whole truck in with them!

Generally speaking drivers of the Eastern bloc avoid big West European truckstops and prepare their own meals from a stock of food stored in lockers. By carrying their own foodstuffs and tools they have an independence and security not shared by other drivers. The Eastern bloc trucker is very keen to safeguard his vehicle and valuable load, because if it should get stolen the state would not think twice about ending his career.

Communist countries tend to rely on West European vehicles for their international haulage. For example, the huge Hungarocamion state-owned transport undertaking in Hungary operates predominantly Mercedes-Benz, Scania and Volvo trucks, although newer Raba 832 and 833 types powered by MAN 256 hp diesels and ZF six-speed splitter gearboxes locally manufactured are used more and more. These vehicles are of a good standard for international haulage, having many parts common to the normal MAN range and so reducing service problems whenever trucks operate in Western Europe.

Another Hungarian truck maker is Csepel, who now market several on- and off-highway types, among which is a modern-looking 6×6 cabover type D-566 with a Raba (MAN licence) 200 hp engine coupled to a six-speed synchromesh gearbox. Highway types include the D-730, which uses an East German Jelcz cab, a Csepel 145 hp diesel, and the type D-469 with 4×4 drive, another DDR cab supplied from the Star factory, but again with Csepel's own 130 hp engine and other running components. Formerly Csepel built cabover Henschels under licence in addition to developing their own conventionals. Hungarian products are exported to other Communist countries and a number of developing African and South American markets.

Romania is the home of the Roman truck – another MAN-licence product – and these trucks are exported not only to Eastern European countries but also to Great Britain and other markets overseas. The state transport company uses many heavy three-axle cabover Roman trucks with either tank- or dry-freight semi-trailers for their international runs, but in addition several old cabover Berliets and Unics are still going strong on TIR work. Romania's other products include the Carpati and Bucegi medium-capacity trucks built at Brasov. These copies of Soviet Zil 150 trucks come with 140 hp V8 engines and are of 4×2 or 4×4 configuration.

Czechoslovakia is by far the best known truck manufacturing country from behind the iron curtain with Skoda, Tatra and Praga all building heavy trucks for home and export markets. The first Laurin & Klement trucks were built in 1905; they later merged with Skoda. Skoda's 706 cabover models have become well known all over Europe due to their extensive use by the CSAD state transport company, which now operates the latest Skoda-Liaz 100.05 and 100.45 trucks. These vehicles are of modern styling and are fitted with 270 or 304 hp six-cylinder diesels and Praga ten-speed gearboxes for gcw of 38 tonnes. Even the colours of CSAD Skodas are now more up to date, the old drab finishes giving way to brighter hues.

The first Czech truck was built in 1900, and the Tatra name was used from 1919. Designer Hans Ledwinka used his central-backbone type chassis-frame first for cars and later for Tatra trucks, and large air-cooled engines first appeared at the end of

Raba 943 tractor built under licence from MAN and operated by the state-owned haulage firm of Hungarocamion of Budapest.

1

World War II. The bonneted 138 range with 6×6 drive has the unique tubular back-bone chassis with power by a 180 hp air-cooled V8 diesel and has found wide acceptance within Communist countries and in Holland, Belgium and France. Another interesting Tatra of the late 1960s was a huge 8×8 or 8×6 heavy haulage or dump-truck chassis, again with tubular construction but with a V12 air-cooled diesel and modern large square cab. Called the 813 this vehicle is also available as a 4×4 tractor with sleeper-cab for long-distance work, and is fitted with a 257 hp V12 driving through a ten-speed gearbox.

Praga is the third familiar Czech truck name but though it has manufactured trucks for a long time current production is geared more to component developing and marketing. Yet many of the latest on- and off-highway models built, such as the V3S and S3 6×6, found a number of customers even in Western Europe. These, with a 95 hp engine were somewhat underpowered chassis and were used predominantly as tippers or mobile workshops.

East Germany (the German Democratic Republic) is the home of Jelcz and Star trucks, of which several examples can be seen in Europe operating on long-distance work, again for the state. Star builds the 28 and 29 medium-capacity highway truck with 105-hp diesel, and in addition a military-type 6×6 off-highway truck. Jelcz, however, is better known and the 315, 316 and 317 types find good use with commercial operators on long-haul work, especially when towing a Jelcz D-830 matching trailer. Grossing at 32 tonnes total, the 200 hp six-cylinder diesel pushes the rig through a five-speed synchromesh gearbox to a staggering 85 km per hour. However 1978 saw the 'birth of a more modern cabover Jelcz with increased power and more driver comfort.

Alongside these locally made vehicles DDR transport operates a whole fleet of drawbar F89 Volvo vehicles, while, for instance, Pekas in Poland uses a mixture of expensive European makes, among which are the newest Saurer D 330 cabover sleepers and F190 double-drive tractors pulling TIR tilt semi-trailers on hauls all over Europe and into the Middle East. Bulgaria is a big user of 'New Generation' Mercedes semis and Berliet TR 280s for their price-cutting international

1. A Yugoslav-built FAP model 18B, powered by a Famos 200 hp diesel, hauls a load of bricks through spectacular scenery in Yugoslavia.

2. Most recent in the Skoda range is the LIAZ 100.45 model which has a 304 hp six-cylinder diesel and ten-speed Praga gearbox.

3. The unusual Tatra 4×4 tractor unit, model 813NT, coupled to a semi-trailer on single tyres. The operator is the state-owned CSAD.

2

3

hauls. An additional factor which has influenced truck types is that Bulgarian drivers have for the past couple of years been employed by the Iranian government to transport goods from West European countries to Tehran in 3,000 new K 1932 Mercedes trucks purchased by the Shah. The agreement is that all these modern semis will become the property of Bulgaria after two years' operations and they will then take their turn on the usual Bulgarian international haul routes.

Truck legislation concerning length and weight limits differs widely between the Eastern bloc countries. For example, Yugoslavia allows a 15 m semi-trailer or 18 m truck-trailer combination to gross at 40 tonnes, whereas Hungary has 14 m and 18 m length limits with 20 tonnes for a semi and 36 tonnes for a drawbar. Bulgaria permits a 16.5 m and 20 m long combination, both with a limit of 38 tonnes. Speed limits for trucks vary from 40 to 60 mph in towns to 70/80 on autoroutes, though the latter is seldom achieved by the local trucks! Because most of the equipment is not marketed in the West, it can happen that Eastern bloc drivers have to dismantle whole assemblies far from home.

THE SOVIET UNION

Only in recent years has the Soviet Union chosen to make public its efforts to improve the quality and quantity of the vehicles manufactured within the Soviet automotive industry. This change of attitude, as far as trucks are concerned, has come about mainly as a direct result of the Russians becoming more export minded, and so new technology has been introduced into the vast Soviet truck manufacturing 'machine' in an effort not only to improve truck designs in general but also to make the vehicles appeal more to export markets.

The Soviet automotive industry is now well over fifty years old, and although some of the current Soviet truck designs still look very dated the manufacturing plants are making rapid strides to catch up with Western technology. Throughout the history of the Soviet automotive industry the number of truck models has always far surpassed that of car models. The reason is simply that trucks are more valuable to the nation's economy, and so truck-building technology has advanced faster than that of the car manufacturing.

The Soviet Union produced up to 180,000 trucks a year before World War II, the majority of the heavier trucks being based on American designs. One such vehicle range, the ZIS-5, was reportedly a much modified Autocar design and remained in production for some thirty years from 1933 to 1963 – a Soviet production record, if not a world-wide one. In 1963 Soviet truck and bus production topped 382,000 units of all types, and by 1973 that figure had almost doubled to 629,400.

In Communist Russia all the truck manufacturing plants are, of course, owned by the state, and so – apart from some small areas of overlap – there is no duplication of model types and ranges, and each truck manufacturing plant will build just one type of truck. Names such as Maz, Kamaz, Zil, Kraz and Uralaz sound strange to Western ears but these are the names of the five heavy-vehicle ranges currently in production. By Western standards most Soviet trucks appear old-fashioned with cab designs dating back to the 1950s which are sparsely appointed inside and have minimum lighting.

The smallest truck in the range of Soviet products is the Zil, which is produced at the Likhachev works in Moscow. This is a two-axle normal-control (or conventional) lay-out truck or tractor vehicle which can gross up to 18 tonnes

when hauling a trailer. The cab of the Zil slightly resembles the mid-1960s Bedfords and is powered by a V8 petrol engine, the same engine which powers the bigger Zil 131A 6×6 off-highway truck, a vehicle which has obvious military uses.

The Uralaz is a recently developed truck range coming from the merger of the older Ural truck range being produced at the Ural Motor Works with some of the Soviet tractor and trailer divisions. Today some twenty-five different versions of the 6×6 truck, tractor and heavy hauling machine are built.

Probably the most versatile truck range produced in Soviet Russia is built by the Minsk Motor Works under the product name of Maz, and these cabover trucks and tractors cover the heavy end of normal highway operations. While the Maz cab design is some twenty years old the vehicles are of very rugged construction and are very long lasting, and in recent years the Soviet Union has been sending Maz hauled rigs on international hauls right across Europe.

The Maz range – all two-axle vehicles – starts with a 5-ton dump-truck or flat-bed and extends right up to a 32-ton gross tractor. A V6 diesel of 200 bhp powers the Maz and this drives through a twin-plate clutch to a five-speed gearbox.

Until lately the Maz was the top heavy-weight highway truck in Russia, but this has been superseded very recently by the Kamaz range of 6×4 cabover trucks and tractors. The Kamaz, which is built with the latest Soviet trucking technology, is a modern and attractive looking vehicle, available with either a 210 or 265 bhp V8 diesel. The Soviet Union's apparent love of V-form engines will by now be very obvious, and this type of engine also extends to trucks built at the Kremenchug Motor Works which are known as Kraz and are built around heavy 6×4 and 6×6 conventional chassis. To Western eyes the Kraz cab looks very similar to the old wartime Diamond T tank transporter chassis, and the Kraz is still built today with a wooden-framed cab. Power for these chunky machines comes from a 265 bhp V8 diesel coupled to a five-speed gearbox which is in

Kraz 257 model 6×2 highway truck for solo or trailer operation. The vehicle is powered by 265 hp V8 diesel and features a five-speed gearbox.

1

2

turn coupled to a high/low transfer box. The Kraz design is one of the Soviet Union's leading exports which are shipped out of Russia through the Soviet Avtoexport Board, which is based in Moscow and is responsible for the export of any motor vehicles from the USSR. The Kraz is offered for sale in Europe, renamed Belaz, and the 256BM dump-truck chassis is proving to be a very sturdy and reliable vehicle; it was the superseded 256B dump-truck which was the first Soviet truck design to be imported directly into Britain via the importer's UMO plant. On the Soviet home market the Kraz range includes heavy haulage tractors, 6×6 dump-trucks and timber tractors, as well as a range of high-mobility cross-country vehicles.

Recently the USSR took delivery of many new trucks which originated outside the Communist bloc group of countries. Many Volvo F89 long-haul tractors were included in the purchase, as were some 9,500 6×4 Magirus Deutz dump-trucks fitted with the well-known air-cooled diesel engine which operates well in the freezing winters experienced in many parts of the Soviet Union. This

3

4

1. The Kraz 256 6×4 tipper is powered by the well-known V8 diesel, and is a popular Russian export.

2. Maz 516B rigid six-wheeler with lift rear axle, exhibited at Gothenburg in 1973. This model has a V6 engine of 200 bhp.

3. Maz 504 articulated outfit engaged on international hauls.

4. The Kamaz is the latest generation of Soviet trucks, and with it the Russians are poised to increase their export-market share.

buying-in of vehicles does not mean that the Soviet Union lacks the ability to build such vehicles itself but serves merely as a stop-gap measure.

While technical information from outside the country is somewhat limited in supply, the most significant trade publications from abroad are available in a couple of libraries in Moscow, and

there is an institute of automotive information, where an army of interpreters and other specialists are kept busy translating the useful portions of the automobile information received from abroad. Supplementing this information, and probably much more useful, are actual studies carried out on foreign vehicles in current production.

Of all the developments on the Soviet truck scene in recent years none can equal the importance and sheer size of the Kama River Plant, the home of the Kamaz truck range. The very latest Soviet technology has gone into this massive plant, which resembles a mini-city in size, on the banks of the Kama River at Naberezhnye Chelny. A lot of the technical knowledge and know-how from the Zil plant went into designing the Kamaz – the Soviet truck of the 1980s – which has resulted in a very pleasing modern-looking truck.

The very first bucketful of earth was moved on the Kama River site back in 1969, and the first items of truck hardware were being manufactured by 1973. When the works is eventually finished it is claimed that it will be able to produce some 150,000 trucks a year and 250,000 diesel engines.

Though much technical information is available on Soviet-built trucks, obtaining facts on actual operating conditions on Soviet soil seems about as easy as getting advance warning of a Soviet moon shot. Trucks operating in Russia are painted utilitarian khaki and get battered into an early old age by icy salty winters and baking dusty summers on generally poor roads. Soviet trucks are devoid of all chrome and of anything else that would make them look fancy or special, and in the hot summers truck drivers tend to discard engine covers, air cleaners and even cab doors in an effort to keep cool. Many truckers can be observed actually hanging out of the door opening, with just one hand on the steering wheel and one foot on the gas pedal while they check their loads on some steep and endless uphill climb. The Soviet truck driver is served by an excellent chain of cafeterias which dispense vast platefuls of soup with sour cream, tomato salad, acid-tasting but excellent black bread and glasses of tea – without milk but with lashings of sugar!

There is real comradeship among Soviet truck drivers in remote areas; pairs can often be seen undertaking major repair work at the roadside, apparently prepared to camp for days if needed.

THE MIDDLE EAST

Always volatile, the Middle East has long been a busy market-place for vehicle builders from both sides of the Atlantic. The recent boom in inter-continental trucking to the ancient world has been jeopardized by far-reaching political and religious upheavals.

Hino six-wheel tanker in typical surroundings.

For many years now an enormous amount of freight has been carried to the Middle East countries. Thousands of tons are shipped to the Arabian ports each week, but only a few ships can be unloaded at one time and long delays and congestion occur which only road transport can solve. Anything from nails to complete refineries are hauled overland all the way to Saudi Arabia, Kuwait, Afghanistan and even Pakistan. These truck-routes must be regarded as some of the toughest and most dangerous in the world, full of adventure and hardship.

The outward run through Europe usually presents little difficulty on well-built highways, but once beyond the Balkans – having presumably mastered the tricky Yugoslavian 'Autoput' highway with its numerous fatal accidents – the real problems arise on the Turkish border. Here road taxes have to be paid and piles of forms completed, with a waiting time often amounting to several days. The Middle East begins beyond the metropolis of Istanbul, which is passed by the Bosporus suspension bridge – at 1,560 m the longest in Europe and a great improvement on the former heavily used ferry.

Worse difficulties are encountered, however, in the south-east of Turkey, where the notorious Tahir mountain range has to be passed to reach the Iranian border. The track consists merely of a badly corrugated and pot-holed loose stone surface, hardly wide enough to allow two trucks to pass, and it winds up the mountains to an altitude of over 2,500 m with inclines of 24 per cent (1-in-4). This stretch is strewn with the wrecks of heavy trucks that ran off the 'road', burned out or simply broke down and were looted by natives. (Disabled vehicles are seldom recovered.) Tracks turn easily into slippery mud paths in snowy winters, while during the soaring summer heat there is dust enough to cover a complete truck. During bad conditions local inhabitants are always willing to give a hand in fitting snow-chains, but if they are not paid sufficient 'bakshish' afterwards knives are very quickly drawn and the incident will cost the driver more than cash alone. While descending the dangerous mountain track in low gear at speeds of only 10 km per hour it often happens that hostile Turks with knives or stones try to jump on the truck and force the driver to stop. Stone throwing and shooting with catapults is a national pastime for Turkish children and a lucrative means of extorting cigarettes or money from truckers; those not complying quickly will find they need a new windscreen.

Trucks operated by a Dutch company, Rijnart Trucks, driving the 20,000 km round-trip to Pakistan, suffer really purgatorial conditions, including temperature variations from −45°C. in winter to +50°C. in mid-summer. The roads are virtually non-existent tracks offering no direction signs whatsoever and bridges too narrow for heavy trucks. The only solution is to ford the river at the shallowest point, but then there is the risk of getting stuck in the middle on some big boulders or of not being able to pull the 38 ton tractor-trailer up the bank on the other side. Rijnart Trucks have used F-model Macks on this haul together with some Scania 140s and more recently a number of specially equipped double-drive tandem Fiat 697T tractors. Trailers are wide-spread tandem flat-beds with strong container-type body-work which gives the best rigidity and protection against the weather, dust and pilfering.

For mutual assistance in case of any trouble most trips are made in convoy, and several other long-distance trucks join in at night to form a strong camp against the possibility of plundering bandits. A trucker ignorant or wilful enough to spend the night alone in the open could consider himself fortunate to be able to drive on alive the next morning.

Loads hauled into Asia consist mainly of radio and television, medical and electronic equipment and all kinds of material for oil companies, such as pipes, machinery, etc. Return loads could be anything from rice or nuts to carpets or copper handicrafts for any destination in Europe.

Truckers have to carry a large quantity of paper-work and cash to negotiate the various customs authorities. They must have available their passport, visa, log-book, international certificate of inoculation against smallpox, cholera and typhoid fever and international or domestic driving licence. Then there are registration forms for tractor and trailer, and the 'Carnet de Passage' – ten copies or more – which speeds up the processes of importing and exporting the vehicle without paying the extremely high taxes which otherwise are only partly recoverable on leaving the country. These are just part of the documents and know-how

1. *A Scammell Constructor 6×6 destined for the Government of Qatar.*

2. *An example of an Iranian-built Mercedes-Benz with the large wheels and tyres and extra fuel tank so necessary for desert journeys. Note sleeper box over cab!*

3. *Iranian-built LS1924, which is used on the long Europe–Middle East route.*

required by the inter-continental trucker, for such things as packing lists, invoices, manifests, etc. concerning the load must also be in order: instances of truckers carrying suitcases for their paper-work are not exaggerated! Some drivers have to be brokers as well, and may have to arrange a return load themselves, which in Pakistan can mean visiting the Minister of Transport himself.

So that drivers may be as self-supporting as possible many trucks are fitted with complete camping facilities, such as a gas cooker, fridge, sink with running water, lockers, and such amenities as air conditioning, stereo radio/cassette recorders or television and a diesel-fuel-burning additional heater against the severe winters.

Mercedes-Benz, DAF, Ford, Volvo and Saviem are a few of the trucks which are marketed with specially designed Middle East sleeper-cab tractors complete with the optional items mentioned. In addition many are fitted with extra spotlights, air-horns, tropical roof, enlarged radiator and sump-guards, while most trailers have a huge 1,000 litre fuel tank slung underneath together with lockers for snow-chains, spares, shovels, etc. Trucks of 300 hp and over are used most widely, preferably with double-drive bogies and sometimes air-suspension on the trailer to give the load more protection on the rough roads. It is hardly surprising that this sophisticated European equipment is stared at in great amazement in Pakistan or Afghanistan, where the colourfully decorated small trucks of bygone days yet make up the scene.

Truckers on Middle East runs can spend up to eight weeks away from home, but the money is good and there is no shortage of applicants for jobs with companies operating to the Middle East. Such a driver must, however, be capable of handling the rig under the worst possible circumstances and be prepared to tackle repairs by himself at the road-side. He must also become a diplomat on the borders and a businessman at the destination.

The big boom in overland transportation to the Middle East has now passed, and several companies have withdrawn their operations – for example British Road Services, who ran a regular service for many years to all parts of the Middle East with specially equipped Leyland Marathons. Others have ventured into new markets even farther afield, and there was speculation that road transport to Singapore would be the next target of

1. MATSS operates this Volvo F89 semi on the difficult services throughout Saudi Arabia, from its base in Jeddah.

2. Seen traversing the deserts of Iraq is this Scania LS140 with TIR trailer.

3. The three-pointed star of Mercedes-Benz has become a familiar sight in all parts of the world and naturally the oil-rich Middle East is no exception to the rule. In this picture a 1632 is seen in operation in Saudi Arabia.

1
2

3

Western European hauliers. This seems doubtful not only because of the even more appalling road conditions of the Far East but also because of the unbeatable government systems and the more than routine interest that local policemen have in Western truck drivers. This special attention is focused on three things: pornography, cigarettes and whisky. Corruption is the order of things too: no money or gifts? no stamps to proceed – that's trucking Asian-style.

Road transport on inter-continental routes will certainly continue, for many Middle Eastern or Asian points are not accessible by ship, and in any case truck freight is generally a lot faster to its destination with less risk of damage or pilfering on the long journey. But the unprofessional and careless 'cowboy hauliers' now think twice before setting off again on the long gruelling trip, and clients in the Middle East have become aware of the better service given by the bigger, experienced truck operators.

With the recent reduction of regular truck traffic to the Middle East many of the intrepid and experienced inter-continental drivers must now roll over the silk-like European highways again for a far lower wage. Some of them chose to stay and work in the Middle East – European-style and affiliated companies have been created in Iran, Syria, Saudi Arabia and the United Arab Emirates, employing European drivers for wages that beat all-comers.

Though road transport has always been a very important business within the Middle East – there being virtually no railways – it was the Europeans and Americans who introduced the techniques and machinery to make the best of local transport needs. So today the majority of truck loads are shared between the established local hauliers and new European-based companies, the latter often using Western vehicles adapted to meet the more severe demands of higher temperatures and appalling roads. The local men still do a lot of carting with old but strong heavy trucks or vehicles built under licence.

The road network in most Arab countries is rapidly improving, with many miles of bitumen laid right across virgin desert, thus giving those trucks of more European specification a good chance of survival, especially if they have additional cooling and air cleaners. The originally imported trucks were (and many still are) specially designed heavy-duty on/off-highway types with many options. Most European, American and Japanese manufacturers are active on these markets, but the lion's share is still for bonneted Volvo, Scania and Mercedes-Benz trucks. In Saudi Arabia in particular the round-nosed Mercedes rigid two- and three-axle trucks are almost the only vehicles seen, with a market share of approximately 80 per cent, and this could increase further now that a completely new assembly plant has been built at Jeddah (in 1978).

Of course there still is a wide variety of manufacturers' trucks, but each is seen in very limited numbers. The Foden Super Haulmaster is selling well, and Macks have always been there alongside International, Oshkosh, GMC, White/Autocar and Kenworth – the last-named in the super heavy-duty oil-field vehicle category. There have been huge 6×6 Kenworth trucks hauling massive equipment through the sand dunes of Saudi Arabia for Aramco since way back in 1956. Both Japanese Hino, Nissan and Toyota trucks can be found all over the Middle East, and MAN, Saviem, Berliet, Magirus-Deutz, DAF, Leyland and ERF are present too. Arab operators have always favoured conventional chassis in preference to cabovers, the former giving a better ride on rough terrain and being initially cheaper and then easier to maintain, while such cabover luxuries as sleeper-cabs are not required on nation-wide hauls. Trilex spoke wheels with a bigger tyre size and off-highway pattern are mostly specified, in order to give a better ride and to improve airflow for cooling around the brake drums and tyres.

Many imported vehicles come complete with body-work or trailers, and this is particularly the case with heavy-duty tippers, tankers, cement hoppers, refrigerated bodies and skeletal trailers – the last-named now being used throughout the Arab countries for traffic from the various ports able to handle ISO containers. Local hauliers with rigid trucks have a preference for high-dropside, stake or fixed-side body-work completed in lively colours and with additional chrome and murals. Many vehicles flourish extra marker-lights, reflectors, flags and other frills to make them stand apart from those of their colleagues and particularly from the mostly plain European company vehicles operating in the Arab world. Several continental haulage firms have subsidiaries in the Middle East,

1

2

3

1. Built for both on- and off-highway use, with its big wheels and short boxvan trailer, this F-series Mack from Iran is heading towards Western Europe.

2. This CCC Centaur cabover 6 × 4 is engaged on the long run from Holland to Teheran.

3. Tempo S.A. of Teheran is the operator of this sturdy looking DAF FTS2600.

for example British Whittrux and Dutch Damco-Van Swieten, both operating Mercedes-Benz 2632 double-drive tractors in Saudi Arabia, while the Arab Saramat and MATSS haulage companies have set up a well co-ordinated fleet of Volvo F89 tractors and trailers, even operating double-bottom outfits consisting of two TIR-type 12 m semi-trailers coupled to the Volvo tractors, all with a strong back-up of European expertise.

Although a number of 'road trains' are used in Saudi Arabia their use is limited to certain stretches. They might seem to be the obvious choice for hauling big loads over thousands of miles of endless desert tracks, but the actual tractor-semi-trailer length limit is 14 m, and 18 m for a drawbar combination with a total gcw for both of 40 tonnes. There seems little uniformity of regulations for truckers throughout the Arab countries – for example an articulated vehicle may measure up to 12 m in Kuwait (though, curiously, the same limit applies to a rigid truck or a trailer outfit), while Iraq permits a 15.20 m articulated truck or a 20 m long drawbar rig. Jordan, Syria and Lebanon have to be content with 14 m and 18 m lengths for each category. These limits are also enforced in Iran with a 36 tonne gcw, but the weights are usually more an indication than an enforced maximum, and overloading is common practice, the driver looking first at the bulk and second at the weight.

Iran is one of the few Middle Eastern countries housing truck manufacturing plants. Though they started with assembly factories both Mercedes-Benz and Mack have come up with almost completely locally produced trucks. The models concerned are of the conventional layout, the Mercedes types L/LK/LS 1924 distinguished by a more angular cab, and Mack R-models by a cab of local construction made by the Kaveh company of Tehran. These have made a great impact on the local truck market, and from time to time some of these very sturdy looking vehicles can be seen picking up a load in some West European port, mostly hooked up to a strong heavy-duty semi-trailer with huge additional tanks underneath and running on over-size tyres. Tempo SA, a Tehran company, is one of these inter-continental hauliers working the Europe–Middle East run from the other end.

In most other Arab countries as well as Iran many distinct old truck makes still roam around,

such as Krupp, Henschel, Diamond T and AEC, and aged Macks of twenty to thirty years ago are yet the hallmark of the Iranian trucking scene. However, the US-built CCC Centaur conventional and Centurion cabover sleeper are unique new additions to Iran not seen anywhere else on this side of the world (though an occasional Iranian CCC tractor-semi-trailer rig might visit Europe on one of its 12,000 km return hauls). In fact Iran is the only Middle East country active in the field of inter-continental haulage, though the range of suitable trucks is wide: Mack F-series, International Transtars, DAF 2800, Mercedes 1932 and Berliet TR 280 models coupled to European-type (Fruehauf) TIR semi-trailers or Strick, Budd or Dorsey American boxvan trailers, with a few locally built heavy-duty types in between, form the majority of haulage rigs driving towards Europe. While many Arab countries now employ European drivers, several, in particular some Dutch, British and West German companies, have hired Turkish truckers to do the inter-continental work. No doubt they are more used to tangling with their home-country customs officials.

Turkey is another country with an exotic truck scene – known to Europeans from the great number of Turkish-registered rigs coming towards most major destinations in Western Europe. Fiat two-axle tractors are common, coupled to long tilt semi-trailers, and impressive Mack F-models, International Transtars and the usual mixture of Mercedes, Volvo and Scania can be seen. However, what at first may appear to be a Scania may in fact be a Turkish-built TOE tractor with double-drive bogie (type 1000), Cummins 350 hp diesel, Fuller thirteen-speed gearbox and a slightly modified Scania 110 forward-control cab. In addition to this home-bred truck Turkey is known for its Chrysler Sanayi-built Dodge conventional trucks (De Soto, US-designed in 1971) which are offered in two- and three-axle form with the Perkins 6.354 diesel coupled to a five-speed synchromesh transmission. These models are very popular in the medium to heavy-duty field where Ford D-series and International Loadstar are strong competitors.

All over the Middle East road transport has become a vital means of making the best use of the oil revenue. Most of this money is spent in the Western world, and the commercial vehicle has a vital role to play.

AFRICA

A whole kaleidoscope of trucks and trucking is contained within this vast continent which embraces so many emergent nations. From the oil-rich north to the copper, gold and diamonds of the south, trucks from all over the world are at work providing transport for the valuable commodities which go to make up the wealth of the continent.

Locally built Ford Traders are used for all manner of tasks in Morocco.

NORTH AFRICA

Another world opens up on setting foot on the African continent, and it is difficult to imagine the relevance of trucks to a landscape in which camels or mule teams are used for ploughing rocky soil and overloaded donkeys stumble by. But the roar of mighty diesel engines is growing steadily stronger and helping to push forward the development of many African countries, not always perhaps in their best interests.

In general the population of North Africa is concentrated along the coastal areas, where some industry has been established, in the large agricultural regions, and at the big harbours of Casablanca, Algiers, Tunis, Tripoli and Alexandria. As there are huge distances to be covered between settlements far inland, and the railway lines are sparse and uneconomic, North Africa is almost completely dependent on road transport, and trucks play a major part in daily life.

Most roads connecting major cities are of a good bitumen standard, while the remainder are either improved gravel or tracks passable in good weather. Of course, the worst stretches are encountered in the more remote parts of the Sahara, where sometimes there are no tracks at all and only old oil-drums or pieces of iron stand to mark the 'road' through endless wastes of stony or sandy desert. Driving is usually very easy with very few other vehicles around, but drivers must always be alert and ready to dodge all manner of carts, cycles and animals in or near built-up areas, with the attendant risk of getting into serious trouble should they hit a careless pedestrian or straying animal. Driving at night is extremely dangerous: there are no white lines on the roads or such novelties as street lamps, yet hundreds of road-users on foot or hoof mix with unlit vehicles of all sizes. Trucks may have a battery of red, green and yellow markerlights all over them but none working at the rear, and the whole vehicle may be piloted by a short-sighted local who has seemingly no other objective than speeding the whole outfit to hell, to judge by his suicidal behaviour on the road.

Passenger transport in Africa is something really special. Old and new buses parade colourful locally built body-work which is not as luxurious as that in Europe but is very efficient and sturdy, often based on a genuine truck chassis to take the punishing roads and driving techniques. These vehicles operate right into the most desolate places and a ride on them will be long remembered. Arabs and Negroes play dominoes while some character climbs out of the window or emergency door to shunt some goods or tie down an animal on the roof-rack, while the bus itself continues to race down a mountain road at break-neck speed. Often more goods – from goats and chickens to carrots and bicycles – are loaded on top of the bus than there are people carried inside. If bus connections fail passengers might hitch a ride on top of a truck load, a sight sometimes seen on many tracks leading into the Sahara desert.

In the case of Morocco and the Spanish Sahara regions big heavy trucks are out of the question on the desert tracks with some very rocky and narrow canyons to pass near the Atlantic coast, and hence small 5-ton capacity Morocco-built Ford Thames Trader conventional trucks, as well as small bonneted Berliets manufactured under licence, are extensively used. Equipped with sand-plates, shovels, jerry-cans for fuel and waterbags of animal skins, these tough vehicles stand up amazingly well against the gruelling conditions, with big overloads of anything from onions and refrigerators to hippies on the top! Driving is done in convoy and usually twice a week on this side of the North African coastal desert, but more inland the heavier trucks play a major part in daily life with a tremendous number of licence-built Volvo N86 and 88 conventional rigid trucks of around 16 tons gross. To enable these trucks to keep on working in southern sand-storms, most are fitted with huge outside air cleaners and invariably come with a loud air-horn: all are of standard dull red colour. Like Volvo, Berliet is also active on the Moroccan market, with assembling of completely knocked down (ckd) parts (engine, axle and other running components) shipped in, and locally manufactured cabs, chassis, etc. fitted near Casablanca. The high content of local parts and assembling is due to the extremely high taxes levied on imported complete vehicles.

Nevertheless a number of more sophisticated trucks have reached African shores, and new DAF 2200/2800, Scania 111, Volvo F88/89 and Berliet TR 250/305 models can be seen today working in Morocco side by side with ancient Deutz, Mercedes, Henschel, Saviem and Bernard trucks, interspersed with a number of old International R-190, Mack LJ/NR and White vehicles. Many of

these individual trucks are in a state of remarkable health and are proudly driven by owner-operators as well as company drivers. CTM of Marrakesh and Satas of Agadier are the main Moroccan transport operators, with both local buses and fully imported luxury coaches, in addition to operating a mixed fleet of vehicles for the carrying of bulk loads or general goods.

Most North African drivers are given to decorating their vehicles with great enthusiasm: cab interiors are often filled with mascots, feminine or religious pictures, bright curtains and numerous smaller items like the well-known little hands which wave when the cab vibrates. Air conditioning is seldom installed: it is probably too expensive, though temperatures in mid-summer can soar up to 50°C. and cooling shadows are scarce, especially on the tortuous trans-Sahara route.

Since the port of Lagos in Nigeria cannot handle half the goods coming in and going out, the most obvious solution for European hauliers was to send the goods over land by truck, and this was being tried by some British companies in 1977. The most recent solution, however, is to ship the merchan-

Photographed in a duststorm, this old Bernard has been given a new lease of life with a DAF engine. It is being unloaded at a small oasis situated in southern Morocco.

dise to the port of Algiers and to continue the onward journey using the Algerian SNTR haulage operator. Although this company had been operating across the Sahara desert for many years, the big boom came in 1978 with an increase in demand from, among others, British Ferrymasters and Dutch Europe Africa Transport, who had investigated road transport overland and come up with SNTR as a likely answer. The 3,600 km one-way haul from Algiers to Kano takes around ten days to complete for a well-trained SNTR group of drivers, who usually drive in convoy but with a respectable distance between vehicles to allow the powdery dust to settle. Clearly this form of trail driving demands a lot of skilful work and an iron constitution, together with the experience needed for dealing with minor breakdowns. The truckers are constantly aware of their responsibility for the

1

2

3

1. A DAF truck chassis forms the basis for this local bus in service at Essaouira, Morocco.

2. Trucks such as this 6×4 Scania 110 Super are well suited to the arduous conditions of operations in the more remote areas of Africa.

3. Overloaded trucks are the order of the day in North Africa, but this enormous load of mattresses is nothing like as heavy as one would imagine.

1

vehicles and their precious cargoes. Thousands of kilometres are unsurfaced and full of corrugations and pot-holes, and there is the ever-present danger of sand creeping into everything. Drivers also have to survive the extreme heat of day and the freezing temperatures of night.

The SNTR operates a 3,000-vehicle fleet of mixed manufacture, among which are 1,200 Mercedes-Benz trucks and tractors of various types, both conventional and the 'New Generation' cabovers with 320 hp V10 diesels which are now favoured for the harsh conditions by both drivers and mechanics. In addition SNTR uses a good number of Berliet vehicles with the TR 250/305 for other long-distance work, while a line of heavy Kenworth off-highway conventionals are operated to supply outlying oilfields and oases. Their success in conquering the desert can be attributed to the fact that this company takes the dangers very seriously and has reliable qualified staff and thorough organizational back-up.

Apart from the ubiquitous SNTR trucks Algeria houses the vehicles of many manufacturers, predominantly French, such as old Saviem, Unic,

Willème and Berliet models plus a number of Volvo and Scania conventional types of various vintages and with many examples of the new N10/12 trucks. Former French colony Tunisia receives surprisingly few vehicles from France, with the exception of Berliet conventional and cabover models; the Italians, however, have invaded with hundreds of heavy Fiat and OM vehicles. Further makes to be seen are Magirus-Deutz conventionals, Mercedes, MAN, old Krupp and Henschel trucks and a number of medium-duty American models by International and Chevrolet. But most impressive are the long-nosed FWD three-axle rigid trucks hauling three-axle full trailers, and the occasional Ford Louisville.

Ford D-series and Bedford normal- and forward-control chassis are strong contenders in the middle-weight class. In Tunisia there is generally a similar vehicle set-up for axles and combinations, like a two- or three-axle tractor pulling a tri-dem bogie Fruehauf semi-trailer, though the so-called tilt TIR body-work is unheard of and most vehicles are either flat-beds or drop-sides. Overloading is frequently seen and failing lights

2
3

1. This Volvo F89 is a 330 hp 6×4 outfit operated by a Dutch haulier on the Holland–Morocco route.

2. An elderly French Bernard with fuel tanks on a flatbed body makes its way from Agadir to Marrakesh in Morocco.

3. Fiats are quite popular in many parts of Africa and they stand up quite well to a variety of tasks. This 682T drawbar outfit is shown operating through Tanzania.

quite common but, on the other hand, loved and well maintained vehicles can be noticed whose operators take great pains to keep the material rolling – with self-made parts if necessary – and many old rigs are consequently still around.

Truckers in these regions certainly do not earn as much cash as their European colleagues, but they do have a valued job which is often the envy of the family and the whole village. As elsewhere the economy depends heavily on trucks to transport the huge loads of supplies – and, in the case of many African countries, to supplement bus services in the more remote areas.

GHANA

Known until 1957 as the Gold Coast, Ghana is famous for its abundant supplies of gold and cocoa. A small rectangular country on the Gulf of Guinea in West Africa, Ghana has most of its population crammed into the coastal areas near the capital of Accra and the major seaport of Tema.

The country is divided almost in two by the huge Volta Lake and River which runs north and south through the country, and this water system has for years provided the means of transportation. However, in recent years a road system has been developed, and trucks have begun to play a more important role in the country's economy.

Although a reasonable road system exists between Tema, the coastal port, and Kumasi, about 130 miles inland, beyond this point most of the roads are little more than dirt tracks. As a result the trucks needed to haul over this terrain are mainly heavy-duty types such as bonneted Mack or Hino chassis equipped with simple drive trains and robust bodywork. Several other truck manufacturers are represented in Ghana, including builders from Europe and Britain.

As with many developing countries Ghana faces an acute shortage of suitably trained mechanics and technicians, and the trucking industry, along with many others, naturally suffers. Consequently, simple engines, such as the Mack Maxidyne, which can be coupled to simple five-speed gearboxes, are found preferable to sophisticated pieces of hardware requiring special driving and servicing techniques. Hino and Mercedes trucks have found favour in Ghana for the same reason.

Despite the recent advances made by the trucking industry the waterways of Ghana are far from redundant. As recently as 1976 a fleet of Mack trucks built in Canada for shipment to Ghana was ordered with many special options to make them suitable for transport aboard the freight ferries which still ply the Volta River system. These trucks, which featured heavy worm-drive rear axles, custom-built drop-side bodies, and which were shipped to Ghana almost full of spare parts, will only accumulate annual mileages of approximately 20,000, with almost double that figure being registered by the ferries on which they will be carried.

1
3

1. Mack R685T Maxidyne-powered dump truck being operated on a road construction project in Ghana. The complete vehicle was shipped from Canada, but without the Bulldog emblem to foil thieves.

2. Mercedes trucks are to be found operating all over Africa, and the bonneted versions are especially popular. This particular dropside truck is operated by the Highways Department in Ghana.

3. One of the more unusual trucks to be found in Ghana is this Saurer cabover heavy-duty rigid.

2

CENTRAL AFRICA

The continent of Africa is one of the most developing and interesting markets for trucks in the world today. Africa is not heavily industrialized but it is rich in raw materials, and with only a very basic and limited railway system trucks are very much in demand for the transportation of freight – and in some cases even people. Many of the trucks found operating there have come as a direct result of political motivations, and vehicles from America, Europe, the Soviet Union and Japan can be found in a variety of shapes and sizes. Although the hot political climate of Africa is forever producing changes of policy, many Spanish-built vehicles can still be seen in the Spanish Sahara region and numerous French Saviem and Berliet trucks in Algeria.

In certain areas all-wheel drive vehicles are still very much needed, with trucks such as the Bedford 4×4, a market leader in this field, although its General Motors parent company is now pouring many American built GMC models into the continent as a whole.

On the Ivory Coast, situated on West Africa's coast-line, drivers employ an apprentice out of their own wages and his function is to keep the rig clean. The apprentice carries a rifle with him and guards driver and rig while the driver sleeps. It is not uncommon to hear of a truck driver found dead with his throat cut and his wallet gone. If the police should ever stop the rig and discover the apprentice at the wheel then the penalty is six years' hard labour for the driver – and a considerably worse punishment for the apprentice!

Because of the political climate of Africa generally there is little unified trucking operation or legislation, and vehicles are often abused, mistreated and neglected by local drivers who often lack a basic understanding of the workings of any mechanical device. There is a tale that has been reported many times in various trucking magazines about the fate of some 200 brand-new trucks of all makes and sizes, donated by various United Nations countries to one particular African state to help out after a national disaster. Within just twelve months all but two of the whole fleet were out of service. Some of the trucks had mechanical failures, often as a direct result of the driver not knowing about checking such basics as oil and water, while others were simply wrecked. There is even the tale of a driver who claimed that a tree

1

2

1. *This Leyland Hippo of the Kenya National Transport Cooperative is seen setting out on the start of its weekly 1,500-mile trip up country.*

2. *A Mack conventional hauling two 20-metre trailers of loose sugar cane back to the processing plant.*

jumped out in front of his truck so he jumped out of the cab quickly, letting the truck crash. Most of the 200 trucks had rear lamp lenses stolen, as it appears that they make ideal food bowls for the natives. This is just an indication of the problems of trying to operate trucks in some of the more primitive areas of Africa today.

Many European trucking companies have in recent years set up operations in Africa after setting up similar and successful operating companies in the Middle East. By bringing skilled mechanics and drivers from Europe to tackle tricky operating conditions the companies stand a better chance of success than if they employed local unskilled labour.

The Dutch heavy hauling specialist company Mammoet has recently been undertaking many heavy hauling jobs right across Africa and has shipped many Mack and FTF vehicles direct from Holland to handle the task. One particular haul to the Kariba Dam, some 2,200 km inland from the port of Dar-es-Salaam, necessitated the fitting of a large 200-gallon water tank to each tractor to provide adequate fresh water for the long trip.

SOUTH AFRICA

Most people would regard the Republic of South Africa as one of the most developed industrialized parts of the continent of Africa today, and yet curiously there are at present no trucks of South African origin being built there. Instead many of the truck manufacturers around the world assemble trucks under licence in South Africa, including Oshkosh, Mack, Ford, International and Kenworth from America; Leyland, ERF and Foden from Britain; and Volvo, Scania, Mercedes-Benz, Fiat, Magirus-Deutz, and Saviem from Europe, while the Japanese Nissan, Isuzu and Hino complete the line-up.

The only heavy truck of true South African design and manufacture to emerge in recent years was the Ralph, built by Rolway Enterprises between 1967 and 1971. Only a few of these hand-built machines were ever built, and although both cabover and conventional tractors were made, and the models incorporated the best tried-and-tested components from around the world, the financial problems of this small manufacturer proved to be insuperable and it became just a name in history.

There have been many major changes and new makes of truck on the South African scene during the past ten years. In 1969 Leyland trucks and buses from Britain claimed a massive 90 per cent share of the South African automotive market; yet by 1973 this had fallen back to 58 per cent, and a special report published in the South African *Financial Gazette* of that year concluded that the Leyland acquisition of AEC vehicles and the subsequent withdrawal of those trucks from the South African market had failed to take into account the high esteem in which AEC trucks were held. Few ex-AEC customers, it seemed, had turned to Leyland, but had purchased elsewhere instead.

By 1977 the Leyland share of the market had fallen to just 13 per cent and sales were even lower for 1978. Leyland is not, however, the only major trucking giant to suffer low sales in South Africa. Kenworth, who entered the South African truck market a few years ago and has a great reputation around the world, managed to sell just two trucks

In the past British vehicles found a ready market in South Africa, but recent political moves have prevented this. Seen here is a 1950s ERF with locally built cab at the head of a short road train.

1
4

2

1. South African Scania 110 with two 20-metre trailers. Note crew compartment at front of body.

2. International ACCO 1800 model with 147 bhp petrol engine loading logs at a railhead.

3. Scania LBT110 tractors are used by this steel haulier. The 'Abnormal Load/Vrag' message and red flags signify an overlength vehicle.

4. Oshkosh is the top-selling American-built truck in South Africa.

3

during the whole of 1977, beaten heavily by one of the smallest and independent truck manufacturers in America, Oshkosh. Oshkosh, who are the leading American truck manufacturer in South Africa, managed to sell 91 trucks in 1977 claiming 1.7 per cent of the market.

Bearing in mind that the overall market for heavy trucks is just 2,000 trucks per annum, the number of models currently available is very high, and so business is very cut-and-thrust. Virtually all trucks are shipped into South Africa in ckd kits for final assembly by South African labour; usually all that originates in the Republic is the window-glass, tyres and batteries.

International Harvester have an unusual line-up of vehicles for the South African market. Apart from the usual ACCO series medium-weight vehicles this includes both the Transtar and Paystar from America, the monstrous Pacific heavy-hauling tractor from Canada, and the 2200 and 2800 series DAF from Holland (which are also sold under the International badge).

The current political situation in South Africa is certainly not helping further expansion in the truck market, and restrictions on fuel supplies and the closing of petrol stations from mid-day on Friday to Monday morning are aimed at keeping the weekend motorist and fuel-waster from the highways. Speed limits were lowered recently to 50 mph on motorways and 35 mph in the suburbs in the interest of fuel saving.

High wages, low taxation and a fabulous climate have attracted people from all over the world to the Republic, either to work or to retire. However, some of the big trucking companies still have problems with staffing senior positions and often have to recruit managerial personnel from overseas. There seem to be few training programmes available in South Africa today.

Vehicle gross weights allow for a maximum of 50,200 kgs and drawbar rigs and double semi-trailer combinations are allowed to be up to 20 m in length. Rigid four-axle vehicles, such as the 'eight-wheeler' can be up to 12.5 m in length, and a normal articulated tractor and semi-trailer rig can be up to 17 m long, but can still haul only a 12.5 m semi-trailer.

The thought of these long and monstrous 50-

1

2

1. British Atkinson was reasonably popular in South Africa.

2. AEC was once quite strong in South Africa. Clan Haulage specified this Mammoth Major eight-wheel rigid as a heavy-duty tractor unit.

tonners might give the idea that South African trucking policy is very liberal, and while pure trucking legislation supports long and heavy-weight equipment, the trucking companies themselves find the going very tough because of the opposition from the South African Railroads. The SAR completely dominates the movement of freight by land in South Africa – and apart from trains it also operates the largest fleet of trucks. Truck operators hauling long-distance must obtain a permit from the Road Transportation Board first, and the RTB works very closely with the SAR, and therefore the railroad is able to ensure that certain restrictive measures are applied to competitive road transport.

Though the SAR dominates the transportation scene it must be realized that it is largely dependent on trucks. The main railroads run around the coast of South Africa and another line runs straight down the centre, but there are no connecting lines in between. These interior regions have to be served by trucks which operate from over 300 railheads, including some thirty in the Johannesburg area alone, many of which operate huge double-trailer rigs for hauling large loads.

Obviously with such an all-powerful and over-bearing body as the SAR to contend with, South Africa is not the ideal place for owner-operators, and yet some do manage to make a living there, often as a direct result of the SAR. The railroads operate on a narrow track gauge of 3 ft 6 in., which is better suited to industrial or light railway operations and so carries a speed restriction which hampers the speedy movement of freight. The carriage of livestock and certain urgent agricultural products is often given to private carriers, the railroad being considered unsuitable for these traffics. Heavy hauling, tanker and dump trucks are also not easily rivalled by the railroads, and some private companies are able to flourish in these sectors of the industry.

LATIN AMERICA

The area abounds with reminders of yesterday's imports from the
United States, but with the emergence of the raw-material nations as
the 'Third World' tomorrow's trucks will be home-produced even if
they bear foreign names.

*Imported Hinos crossing a bridge in the Panama
Canal zone.*

Transportation problems are enormous in South American countries. Great distances have to be covered on roads rarely of a good all-weather standard and in a demanding climate. Brazil, for example, has a width of 3,000 miles and contains impenetrable rain forests through which only a limited number of roads have been built and these still primarily of a red-earth graded structure which turns into a knee-deep quagmire as soon as the heavy rains fall. Many truckers will fit chains to wheels to conquer such stretches and also carry plates, shovels and even axes to build primitive bridges of logs to cross impassable streams during the rainy season. The Trans Amazone Highway linking the east coast of Brazil with Peru, a distance of almost 4,000 miles, is being bulldozed rapidly through dense jungle and constructed with an improved all-weather surface of bitumen, but many rivers have to be bridged, and until this is done truckers have to rely on very fragile ferries made of nothing more than a bunch of huge logs. These ferries ply between such steep riverbanks that mechanical shovels or bulldozers are needed to pull heavy-loaded vehicles off the 'raft'.

The opening of the vast tropical rain forest regions is a necessary step towards colonizing the isolated native population and further developing the natural riches found in quantity below the surface. Millions of dollars have been spent on the construction of new roads and freight-terminals outside major towns, and yet thousands of miles are added annually in preference to the very inefficient railway system. Vast tonnages are thus transported by road, and in consequence Brazil permits a 40 tonne gcw for a truck and drawbar trailer combination within an overall 18 m length, and a 39 tonnes gross for a 16.50 m tractor-semi-trailer outfit with five axles, or a gcw of 32 tonnes for a British-style four-axle articulated truck. Recently many semi-trailers with tri-axle bogies have been added to road fleets, but the majority of vehicles consist of rigid two- and three-axle trucks with a 22 tonnes gvw maximum and 12 m. length.

With over 90 per cent of the Brazilian road network still unpaved, and many old routes with poor

A bright new Volvo truck overtakes the much longer-established and more colourful local transport in Peru.

1

foundations and simple wooden bridges, the axle
weight limit of 10 tonnes for a single or 16 tonnes
for a bogie is quite generous. While the law is fairly
strict in its insistence on weight and length limits,
and on the wearing of seat-belts in a truck and the
carrying of a fire extinguisher, there are no rules
limiting driving hours or regulation of haulage
permits. On the other hand rates per ton-mile are
State-controlled.

Trucking within the boundaries of Brazil is
difficult enough and drivers are away from home
for up to a month, clocking up to 5,000 miles
return. The international hauls are even more
demanding: Brazilian truckers regularly conquer
the snow-clad 3,000 m-plus passes of the mighty
Andes mountain range on their way to Peru or
Bolivia, while others drive down to Uruguay and
Argentina hauling tropical fruits or industrial
materials. Many of the goods coming in or out of
major cities, which have a ban on trucks during the
daylight hours, are transferred and stocked at terminals in the suburbs – one of the newest and
biggest complexes is the Terminal Rodoviário de
Cargas do Brasil near the capital Brasilia in the

2

1. A Volvo N10 picks its way carefully along a
narrow mountain road with overhanging rocks.

2. Built under licence from International Harvester,
the Dina is a popular medium-weight truck in
Mexico.

3. Scania Brasil build a comprehensive range of
heavy trucks for the South American market. This
110 conventional is typical of those operated locally.

heart of the country. This terminal occupies an area of 1,200,000 sq.m and accommodates a grand total of seventy-one transportation companies with additional facilities for staff and visitors plus a 200-unit motel for truck drivers, a large restaurant and parking lot for over 500 trucks. Not many of these ultra-modern facilities are found in South America, and truckers usually rely on small roadside cafes or stay with their vehicles and prepare their own meals, sleeping in the cab or underneath the trailer.

Brazilian truck production amounts to around 80,000 vehicles a year, of which 30 per cent are gasoline-powered and in the medium capacity range. With the rising cost of fuel around the world there is a strong tendency towards the use of diesel-powered vehicles, and both Cummins and Detroit Diesel are popular conversions to gas-powered American chassis. With a total of almost 40 per cent of the truck market Scania do Brasil is favoured by both small and large hauliers in Brasil and exports to many neighbouring countries, including Mauritania, Angola and Mozambique in Africa. The first Scania's – type L 65 – were

imported in 1951, and many of these faithful old warriors are still seen on Brazilian roads today. Scania now offers a vast line of commercial vehicles and stationary or marine diesel-engines with the basic models being the conventional L/LS/LT 111 and 350 hp LK and LKS 140 cabover, which has a set forward front-axle to comply with local axle weight laws. The last fully imported Scania was delivered in 1957 and from that time trucks were assembled with a very high local content in a 85,000 sq.m manufacturing plant giving work to over 3,000 people. The importance of the plant is shown in the fact that several parts, including all the oil pumps used in Scania trucks around the world, come from Brazil.

Forward-control sleeper-cab versions are relatively new to South America, but both Scania and Mercedes-Benz have always offered – and still do – an adapted sleeper extension on their heavy conventional series, which are the backbone of Brazilian and Argentinian long-distance transport. Production at Mercedes-Benz do Brasil amounts to approximately 30,000 trucks annually, ranging from the little L 608 to the LS 1929, all normal-

3

control models. Mercedes trucks and buses have been assembled in Brazil for many years now and are exported to many other Latin American countries. Many medium-capacity L 1113–L 1513 types are shipped to the United States, where they are helping the fuel crisis by ousting the thirsty gas-guzzlers. As in the US diesel power is more in demand by Brazilian hauliers, but many Chevrolet, Dodge and Ford trucks are still gas-powered.

The heaviest Dodge marketed by Chrysler of Brazil is the 900 series with a gvw of 22.5 tons and powered by a 196 hp V8 coupled to a five-speed gearbox, synchromesh optional. Chevrolet offers locally manufactured trucks with two or three axles and optional all-wheel drive as the C 60 series powered by a six-cylinder 151 hp gasoline engine for gvw of up to 19,500 kg. Ford, however, produces in addition to its gasoline-powered models the F 600 with a 140 hp diesel engine and with three axles grossing at 19 tons.

Fabrica Nacional de Motores (FNM) have produced from 1969 onwards the Alfa-Romeo type 900 and 950 trucks and tractors, which were only recently updated with more modern forward-control cabs and Cummins diesels, made in Brazil, fitted as optional. Most American manufacturers, such as General Motors, Ford and Chrysler are also assembling medium-capacity trucks in other Latin American countries, while Fiat has a large plant in Argentina and builds a whole range of cabover models with the 260 hp 697 N as its maximum

This LK140 is one of the models built to local requirements by Scania Brasil. Note the set-forward front axle, 22-in. American-type wheels and extra window in cab.

weight chassis. Volvo is another manufacturer strongly attached to Latin America with both conventional N types and cabover F models selling well in Peru and Chile, while Mack has set up an assembly plant in Venezuela to build conventional R models. The Japanese, and in particular Hino and Nissan, have arrived in force lately, and Spanish Pegaso and Barreiros have been in the game for a long time – no surprise considering the former Spanish influence.

Most trucks look well kept despite the often murderous roads and weather conditions, and owners show a lot of pride in their trucks as can be seen from the gaily decorated wooden bodywork and double chromed bumpers with little flagstaffs on each side, and a row of coloured marker-lights and hand-written mottoes or names.

As in South America the operating conditions in the countries of Central America are arduous, with roads climbing from sea-level to 3,000 m in places and where the ambient temperature can vary from 40°C. on the coast to 15°C. up in the mountains. In Guatemala, El Salvador, Honduras and Mexico most trucks are in the hands of owner-drivers, and companies with a ten-vehicle fleet are regarded as big. Many of the small hauliers handle their own maintenance and carry out complete overhauls.

There is on average little inter-country road transport, though some trucks from El Salvador may drive into Mexico as far as Vera Cruz to deliver bananas.

Mexico is the only country which houses two truck manufacturers, of which Ramirez, built by Trailers de Monterrey, is best known. This company has been in the business for several years, having started as a trailer manufacturer, but now – in addition to a range of full- and semi-trailers – it also produces jeeps, heavy trucks and buses. The Ramirez second-generation conventional tractors and trucks with two or three axles, designated the R20 and R22, are powered by a Cummins NTC 335 coupled to a Fuller RTOF 915 gearbox and have a maximum gcw of 36 tons in Mexico. These models are unique with cabs built locally to a Ramirez design and distinguished by a forward-hinged hood with bull-bar and an aerodynamically shaped cab with extrusions in both doors to allow a driver to sleep cross-ways on a bed made by arranging the driver's and co-driver's seats. This company does not completely shun new designs in vehicle con-

The Dina and Ford medium-duty trucks are seen here waiting for a load of bananas in El Salvador. They are typical examples of the local trucks.

struction, however, as can be seen in its luxury coach model with four axles, the TM 44, a twin-steer eight-wheeler with raised deck of 13.21 m length and a total weight of over 15 tons. Power is by Detroit 8V–71.

The second Mexican manufacturer of trucks is Dina, who produce light to heavy vehicles with cabs based on various International models. The Dina 3000 on the lower end is powered by a six-cylinder VAM gasoline engine, while the heavier medium-capacity 500 and 600 series, similar in appearance to International's Loadstar, are powered by Cummins V6 and V8 diesels up to 210 hp for a gvw of 13,500 kg. A Cummins NH 250 powers the heavy tractor in the 661 series, which model sports a modified Fleetstar cab, but top of the range is the 861 three-axle tractor (Transtar conventional cab) for a gcw of 41 tons and powered

by the Cummins NTC 350 coupled to a twenty-speed Spicer gearbox! In the past Dina heavy trucks were fitted with slightly modified Diamond Reo conventional cabs, but when these models were discontinued in the United States the company decided to obtain the complete range of International conventional cabs. In addition to these two genuine Mexican breeds both Ford and General Motors build medium-duty trucks under licence, the majority gasoline-engined.

Other makes imported in these regions are a number of US-built heavies such as Kenworth, White and Mack, while in addition to a few Europeans, Mercedes-Benz, Magirus-Deutz and Fiat plus Swedish Volvo and Scania, the Japanese have another strong arm with Hino, Toyota, Nissan and Mitsubishi all selling in quantity. The fast rate of development and industrialization in these Latin American countries means that a tremendous increase in commerce, both within the nations and with foreign countries, is taking place. Railways are of limited importance, and the Latin American truck operators, small or large, will have to continue to link producer and consumer.

CUBA

The transport scene in Cuba is probably the most interesting in the world today simply because of the variety of equipment used there.

While the list of truck types there is not endless and does not match, for example, the tremendous variety of marques found in Belgium, the country is unique in that there is a complete mix of Soviet, East German and American equipment, with a smattering of other types from Central and South America.

The reasons for this highly unusual situation are fairly obvious. Until 1959, when Fidel Castro overthrew the government, Cuba's biggest trading partner was the United States, on which it relied almost entirely for most finished commodities. As a result most cars and trucks used in Cuba pre-1959 were of US origin, and Mack, White, International, Ford, Chevrolet and others dominated the haulage world there. A growing road network spread out gradually from commercial and industrial centres such as Havana and Santiago de Cuba as the Americans grew to appreciate the importance of Cuba's huge nickel reserves. And sugar,

1. This Nissan cabover and trailer is about the largest type of vehicle operating in Cuba. It is pictured here hauling goods from the dock area of Havana.

2. This AC model Mack is one of a group of fifty-year-old veterans still working. Note the chain drive, crank-handle starting, and full air conditioning! Extras gathered over the years include the 'west coast' mirrors, heavy-duty front bumper and sheet rack.

Cuba's biggest natural resource, was used to help finance this American interest.

Shortly after 1959 the United States withdrew all support from Cuba, and in 1961 all relationships were terminated. With almost no finished goods coming into the country Castro looked around desperately for an alternative source of supply. The country that came to his aid was, of course, the Soviet Union.

Initially the flow of goods from the Soviet Union into Cuba was barely more than a trickle. Elderly Maz, Gaz and Kraz trucks were shipped over to shore up the trucking industry. These were supplemented by vehicles such as the Praga and Tatra from Czechoslovakia, the IFA and Grübe from East Germany, little Stars from Poland, and Ebros and Barreiros from Spain.

At the same time as this was taking place Cuba, realizing that for many years it would not have enough finished goods of any description, began looking in its own backyard for equipment. A massive resurrection began, and trucks and cars that had been put out to pasture many years earlier began a new and useful life under the Castro regime. The era of 'waste not, want not' inspired everyone, not just the poor peasant community. Trucks were rebuilt by cannibalization, fabrication and bastardization, but many thousands became road-worthy once more.

As a result of these moves the visitor to Cuba today can still see many examples of American trucks from the 1950s, 1940s, and even the 1930s. In fact in 1978 a fleet of no less than six AC model Macks, complete with chain drive and original cabs and engines, was still working in Havana. These were almost certainly over fifty years old! Many trucks are almost unidentifiable, having modified cabs or bodywork; many others display the wrong nameplate.

In Cuba today the trucking industry looks healthy. The many old warriors from the United States and the Soviet Union have been joined by modern Fiats and Mercedes from Argentina, Pegasos from Spain, Nissans and Hinos from Japanese plants in Central America and bonneted Berliets, presumably direct from France. The Soviet equipment has changed too and in place of the tiny Maz and Gaz trucks which once were the sole representatives of the Soviet Union in Cuba, one now sees heavy Kraz 257s and 258s together with many Zil 130s and Maz 504s. The scene is varied indeed.

2

3

1. *A heavily laden Grübe, built in East Germany, passes by the Capitol Building in Havana.*

2. *This Kraz 258 is typical of the heavier trucks imported from the Soviet Union. Non-standard fitments include the V8 symbol, fog lamps and headlights. Note the useful opening windscreen and decorations on the bumper.*

3. *Another East German import is this tiny Robur panel van seen in a Havana street.*

THE TRUCK HOBBY

The truck hobby has risen in the last few years from almost obscurity to the fastest-growing sector of the vehicle interest market. Clubs, books, models, restorations and rallies all serve to underline the ways in which the enthusiast is being catered for in this fascinating branch of transport.

Truck models, photographs and catalogues are just some of the items collected by truck hobby buffs.

SPECIAL PURP

TRUCK TRAC

SEMI-TRAILER TRACTOR & LOGGING TRACTOR

G.C.W. 34,000kg(

5TH WHEEL LOADING CAPACITY : 8,500kg

CF

CONSOLIDATED FREIGHTWA

Truck enthusiasts or buffs, like the trucks they enjoy, come in all types, and pursue their interest from many different angles. With some it is truck models, with others truck photographs and literature, and with many it is truck driving. Talk to one man and you'll find he is mad on heavy haulage, turn to his friend and he will tell you about the time he chased an old Mack half-way up the motorway. One will be turned on by big glorious posters of Kenworths and Peterbilts, while another will go round yards collecting fleet numbers.

As we say, it's all a matter of taste. This is clearly seen at a club meeting, for in one corner you will find several people gazing at finely detailed models of bright new artics, while a few paces away a group is in a huddle over a box of catalogues and other goodies. Suddenly the lights go down and there's a scramble for seats for a slide show. Once it starts you can be sure of some comments from the audience, for nobody sits for long without uttering a remark, although they vary from whoops of delight at a real tough old truck to derisory and ribald comments at an over-restored vintage truck. Too many slides of everyday Fords and Bedfords raises the old slow handclap, or members start to talk among themselves. But bring along a box of twenty-five-year-old trucks together with a sprinkling of heavy haulage rigs and a few off-beat trucks from faraway places and the audience is yours.

When did all this interest in trucks begin? Transport has always had a following of enthusiasts, although truck fanatics are about the last link in the chain, so to speak. There cannot be said to be a long history of lorry enthusiasts stretching way back, as there is with the more glamorous ship, railway and aircraft subjects. If one can measure the amount of following for a hobby by the amount of literature that is generated about that subject, then we find that, with the exception of trade journals and technical books, the truck enthusiast of pre-war days was not considered to exist. Even in the twenty years or so after the war commercial vehicle enthusiasts were pretty thin on the ground, and little was available to whet their appetites. If you were a dedicated enthusiast in those days it was still very much an uphill battle to gain recognition, for there was adequate publicity for 'train spotters', 'aircraft loggers' and racing car followers, but why on earth should anyone be interested in lorries!

Well we can console ourselves that the tide has at last turned in our favour. Manufacturers, operators, publishers and many drivers know of our existence, and a whole flood of books, magazines, posters, photographs, models and other paraphernalia is now available. One can now glance at the Volvo clock, put on a Bedford T-shirt, button up the Scania jacket, doff a Foden cap, pin on a Scammell badge, tighten up the old Peterbilt belt buckle, grab a DAF holdall, pick up a Mercedes ball-point, mark off the Leyland calendar and kiss goodbye to that gorgeous girl on the Kenworth poster!

And there's another thing about the truck hobby – it appeals to young and old alike – and applies equally to old and young trucks! Some young guys go bananas over huge American rigs all sparkling and resplendent in their multi-colour extravagance, while other older types will quietly search out details of some obscure little firm which built three-wheelers in a back-street in Berlin. Naturally it is the big powerful trucks which make most of the running, and most of the truck 'goodies' currently available are slanted in that direction. One can get belt buckles, posters, stickers, patches, models, place mats, caps, T-shirts, jackets and grips – all with North American-type trucks used somehow. True, there are a few small models available of other countries' hardware, but nothing of the same scale or detail of some of the American plastic kits in the larger sizes. Some manufacturers outside the United States have also prepared a variety of publicity items which are eagerly sought after by truck fans. These include the usual ball-point pens, ashtrays, badges and wall posters which are common enough, but now and then someone comes up with a really good model or detailed company history book.

One important thing about trucks to their enthusiasts is their variety. No matter where one lives one is bound to see vehicles of some kind (leaving aside some tiny islands or the Antarctic). Of course the numbers seen can vary from hundreds an hour on the busiest routes down to one a day in some outlandish places. Another attraction is the unexpected, and one is often surprised to find some trucks far away from home, for unlike buses trucks do not usually ply a regular route at specified intervals – not that all buses do either!

Ever since the vintage car movement got into its

An AMT 1/25th-scale kit was the starting point for this Australian prototype Kenworth five-axle rigid with drawbar trailer carrying removable ISO-type containers.

stride in the 1950s there has been a parallel if lesser interest in old commercials. The forming of the Historic Commercial Vehicle Club in Britain in 1957 gave fresh impetus to the vintage truck and bus collecting fraternity, and similar organizations now exist in many countries of the world. The immediate supply of very old vehicles has probably petered out now and those dragged unwillingly from barns and hedgerows today are of much later origins. However, undismayed, the collectors have cast their nets ever wider, taking in most of the countries of the free world and still discovering some rarities.

Once rescued, some of the vehicles never reappear – for often the task of restoration proves to be more expensive and time-consuming than was at first thought. Others duly make an appearance at old vehicle rallies, lovingly rebuilt and cared for by their new owners. As with so many other things, the vehicles one sees at rallies are not always a fair selection of the vehicles that once graced our highways. Some marques seem to have enjoyed a far higher survival rate than other equally well deserving models, but again we all have our personal preferences about what ought to be preserved.

The purists will also point out that many vehicles seen at the various meets do not present themselves in their working state, for some tend to be 'over-restored', for want of a better description. Still, they do actually run and make appearances for all

to see them, which is far better than keeping them locked up in a building without ever turning a wheel. But then again some of the exhibits are irreplaceable if damaged, and one can understand the owners' reluctance to rally them.

Probably the height of old vehicle culture is reached by those individuals who succeed in not only restoring their vehicles and taking them to rallies, but who also actually use them for work as in their original state. With so much of current legislation aimed at preventing these old vehicles from being operated, it is indicative of their owners' resolution that they ever manage to get them back into service, after having carefully picked their way through the vehicle legislation minefield. Few enthusiasts would wish to see a wholesale return to trucks of the 1920s with solid tyres, oil lamps, clash-type gearboxes and two wheel brakes, though it is good to see occasionally some veteran of a past generation gently going about its business amid the swarm of sheet-rust and plastic of everyday traffic. Notice also the effect an old vehicle has upon other road users: it generates a lot of goodwill and even the traffic police smile! These features have been noticed by some enterprising individuals, for replica delivery vans are now available which demand attention for the van and its business.

For the truck enthusiast who wishes to have his own fleet, some entrepreneurs are only too happy to oblige, and not at too high a cost, for the world of model trucks is another extension of the hobby which is rapidly expanding. Actually models are almost as old as the vehicles themselves, for it was soon after internal combustion engined vehicles first took to the road that models started to appear. In this context the word model includes all kinds of small reproductions of the real thing, for most of the early models were in fact children's toys made either in wood or metal.

As one would imagine, model or toy trucks have appeared in many forms, sizes, scales and materials, from rather crude plain wooden toys capable of withstanding the worst treatment from small children, through the mass-produced tin-plate and cast-metal variety up to the custom-built finely detailed scale model.

Some of the early tinplate toys were really works of art, being well-proportioned recognizable copies of the originals. The method of applying the

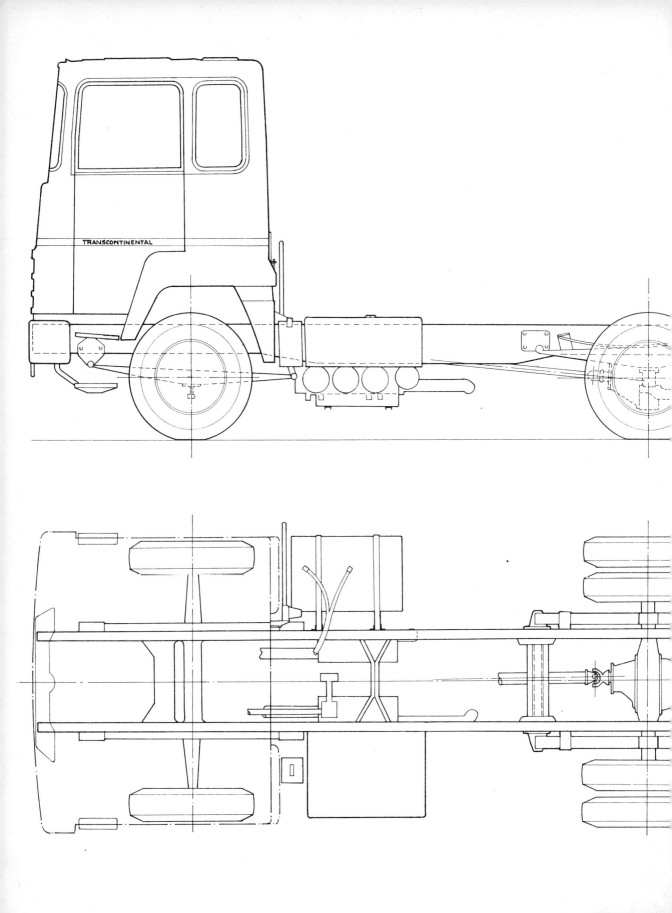

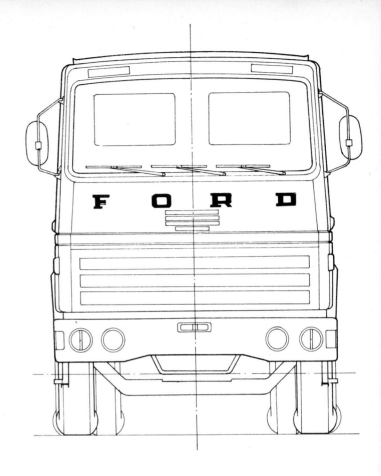

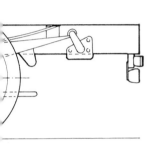

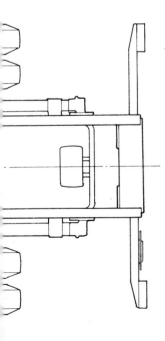

FORD TRANSCONTINENTAL 4 × 2, 3937mm WHEELBASE

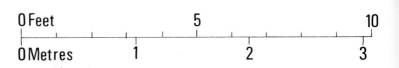

1. *There are many old Diamond T wreckers still in use in Britain, but none so smart as this 1/25th-scale special built from a plastic kit.*

2. *Nicely 'weathered' and positioned on a forest 'road', this model of a Mack conventional logging outfit is normally kept in a glass case, well away from the builder's inquisitive children!*

1

2

painted finishes was extremely good, for often these toys had to withstand some pretty rough treatment at the hands of successive children as they were handed down through the family before being consigned to the attic. These old models have become 'collector items' and are eagerly sought after by some. But the real truck enthusiast is more concerned with better representations than were achieved by the earlier toys. For him it is the later die-cast metal or plastic models or kits which represent the best investment for his leisure hours. Luckily there is an ever-widening choice of scale, detail, subject and price, for the model truck hobby is expanding.

Some modellers are really no more than collectors, for they obtain all the ready-built models which take their fancy, their choice perhaps being ruled by such considerations as scale, vehicle type, country of origin, amount of detail, or perhaps price. The next step is the man who buys ready-built models but then repaints them into either a more accurate copy of an operator's livery or one of his own choosing.

Then we come on to the modeller who limits himself to altering and improving the original model. This can take many forms, from merely replacing the toy racing car type of wheels for something more in keeping with a heavy truck, right up to scrapping all the model with the exception of the cab which then forms the starting point for something better. Within this section there is plenty of scope for 'customizing' the original model, although this term has become connected with the art of painting in jazzy colours and fitting wide wheels and fur linings to small vans, which is not what is meant in this context. According to their taste some modellers alter the original by dressing it from the top as it were, by cleaning up the body and adding extra detail such as ladders, walk-ways, grab handles, mirrors, loads, sheets, ropes, air hoses, trailer couplings, number-plates, cab windows, etc. Some like to add interior detail to the cab, and most like to fit better wheels and tyres. In some instances the body is removed and another substituted, or a rigid is converted into an articulated tractor. With this level of alteration the original 'chassis and axles' unit is retained along with the cab, and the next step is that of dispensing with the chassis/axle unit, for often this bears little resemblance to a real chassis layout.

As mentioned earlier there are some modellers who buy the model only for the cab, for this is the item which is most difficult to construct from scratch, particularly if it is one of the older rounded style of cab, with no flat panels. On the other hand, the chassis frame is reasonably straightforward with the usually straight and parallel side rails spaced with several cross-members.

It is at this stage that the 'remove and replace' level of modelling moves into a much more detailed and involved form, for we are now entering into the realms of 'scratch-building' perhaps almost the whole model. If we use a rigid chassis, non-flexible springs and fixed axles, then we must get the whole assembly square and parallel – otherwise some wheels will be off the ground.

Upon the mention of wheels most modellers prick up their ears, for good scale wheels are often the most important item leading to a well proportioned model. They are also the most difficult item to obtain. Many of the mass-produced die-cast models which form the basis for conversion-type modelling come with rather plain and wrong-size wheels. Often they are merely singles all round when they should be twins or duals at the rear. Another problem is that they are often the same disc type at both front and rear, in other words without any off-set. This can sometimes be conquered by fitting fancy discs or nave plates which were popular some while back, but this looks rather out of place on a dump-truck. Other problems with wheels are that they are often of one size for several different models, usually they have no centre detail, and often they have the wrong section tyres fitted. In the very small (HO/OO) sizes of model the wheels are often too wide in section – they look more like Formula 1 racing strips!

Closely allied to the problem of wheels is that of axles and springs. Should the wheels be free to revolve on the axle or should the axles be fixed to the wheels and turn within an outer axle tube? Or do the wheels need to revolve at all? The fixed wheel and axle arrangement is a lot easier to fabricate especially in the smaller scales. Road springs can be fabricated from many layers of material for authenticity or cut from the solid with scoring for the leaves, again it is a matter of personal choice, weighing up accuracy, time and ability. Often the most difficult part is fabricating the spring hanger brackets and attaching them both to the springs

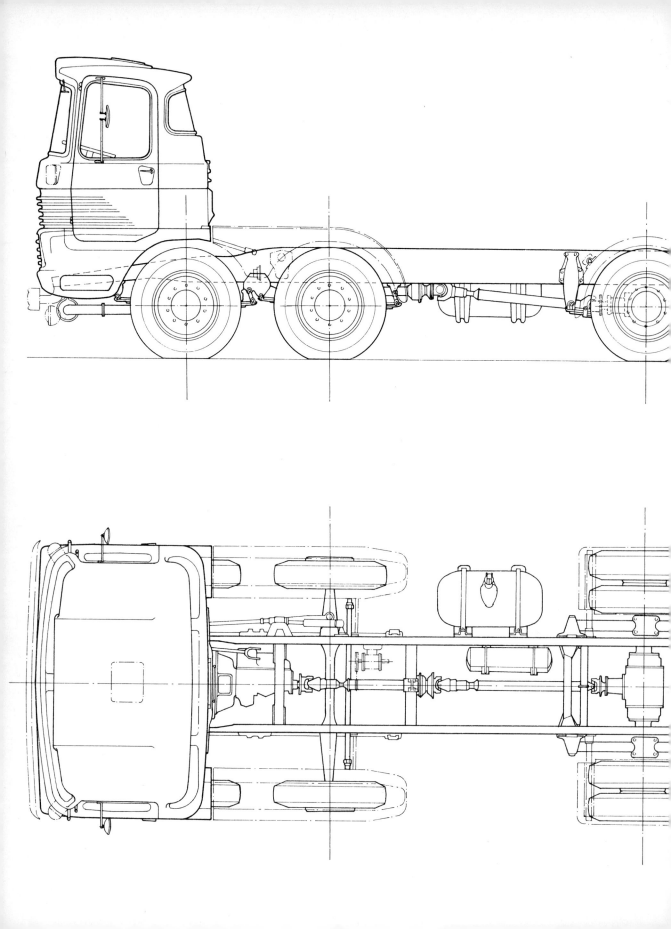

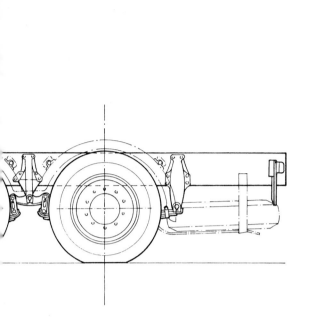

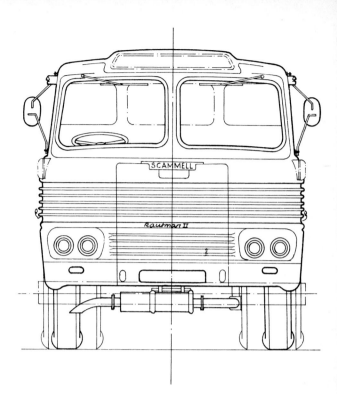

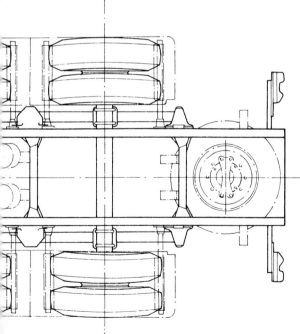

SCAMMELL ROUTEMAN MK II, 16ft 0in. WHEELBASE

0 Feet   5   10

0 Metres   1   2   3.

and to the chassis frame squarely.

Some of the kits which have come on to the market in recent years have opened up new horizons for truck modellers everywhere. The range of scales, variety of types and choice of price provides scope for all, whether it is for just one highly detailed example in $\frac{1}{25}$th scale or a whole fleet in 4 mm. One drawback is that British and European prototypes tend to be in the smaller scales, while the larger scale has predominantly US-style rigs. Any modeller worth his salt is not put off by this, however, for the longer he models the greater the scope for varying the kit by changing parts and scratch-building those he needs. The present practice of manufacturers producing kits based on home-country prototypes will soon disappear as the hobby gains more followers, and many modellers soon progress to buying the kits merely to get the wheels, axles, springs and other parts readily available, and they then go on to scratch-build the rest.

Whether he buys a particular kit because of the scale or because of the subject is up to the individual. Usually the scratch-builder or kit converter adopts a certain scale and sticks to it regardless of prototypes offered. If they don't sell it then he'll go ahead and fabricate it from whatever is available. Naturally cost, time and storage space come into the choice of scale in one way or another, because it is far easier in terms of space and cost to assemble a whole fleet in $\frac{1}{48}$th scale than in $\frac{1}{25}$th. On the other hand, if you want to put your finished models in a scale setting such as an industrial complex or railroad yard then you are much more likely to choose HO/OO scale.

The widespread use of plastics in the period since about 1950 has been of great assistance to modellers, for before that there was only cardboard and wood, obeche and art board, dowelling and cigar boxes. Nowadays, with the possible exception of wheels and tyres, plastics are easy to acquire and simple to use, and by the careful application of heat they can be coerced into many forms useful in the construction of small parts and fine detail. Model shops will gladly supply sheet, tube, rod, angle and other shapes of varying thickness and size. If you care to look elsewhere there are many other shapes and mouldings which will lend themselves to manipulation and conversion. In addition there is an almost never-ending array of everyday

Roy Chapman of London created this impressive drawbar tanker outfit by carefully modifying and adding to the AMT kit of the International Harvester cabover. Tank bodies are cut from a length of drainpipe!

plastic containers that the serious modeller will be able to make use of for something or other. Obvious ones are washing up liquid bottles or rainwater pipes for tankers, smaller tubing for air cylinders, shirtbox acetate for windows and thick rubber tubing for tyres.

One problem which often besets scratch-builders isn't so much building the model as getting adequate information in the first place. Ideally a scale drawing marks the start of a project, while photographs and a note of the colours used is helpful. With current vehicles it is comparatively simple to acquire drawings and photographs, but it is with older vehicles that problems can arise. If no example of the original vehicle has survived one may have to work from meagre information such as a magazine photograph plus the wheel-base dimension and perhaps someone's faded memory of the colour-scheme.

If you can find an example of the vehicle then it's all down to recording measurements, although photographs can still be useful to refresh the memory about a particular point, not forgetting a view from above. The cab is usually the most difficult part to measure accurately, for pressed steel or plastic moulded cabs contain a lot of compound curves which it is extremely difficult to get on to paper. Luckily most of the very old vehicles had almost rectangular cabs so the problem is not so great. Remember that if you do use photographs for reference a long-focus lens gives a less distorted image, but trying to get a dead side view from which to scale off dimensions can also prove difficult. One organization with a large fleet used always to photograph their vehicles from front and side, and carefully included a long stick marked in feet: very thoughtful of them!

Painting, lining and lettering is something which requires special care, for it is these final stages which can wreck all the hours of patience and skill spent in construction. Nothing spoils a model more than a poor finish. Better to have the vehicle in flat grey primer rather than attempt a fancy colour scheme and make a hash of it. Some modellers have acquired the skill to finish their models in a finely executed livery, while others call upon painting specialists to give their work a professional finish.

Often the secret of a good finish is to use one of the miniature spray guns on the market and to use a paint which dries with a matt or semi-matt finish. Accurately matching the paint to the original colour is also important, and avoiding overspray on other parts, especially windows, needs accurate masking and constant vigilance. It is a real artist who can accurately line and letter a small-scale model, although the commercially available decals and lettering are indispensable to many of us. The positioning and spacing of lettering is as important as having it the correct size. One particularly tricky situation arises when the lettering is arranged in a gentle curve such as was common on many truck cab doors or across the cab front, and meticulous preparation to ensure a smooth curve and regular spacing will be well rewarded.

Finally the presentation of a model is all important if the correct atmosphere is to be achieved. Included under this subject of presentation will be the display of the model, its location within an overall setting and the use of accessories to help create the desired effect. The majority of truck models are displayed in splendid isolation, i.e. just as they are or perhaps mounted on a simple wooden base. For convenience and safety some are kept in display cases, particularly the larger models which cannot be put in the family glass cabinet and those which are frequently taken to exhibitions. Other models are sometimes used as part of a larger overall model such as in the yard of an HO/OO scale railway layout. Sometimes these models are dressed up with loads such as barrels, drums, timber or containers in an effort to justify their presence in what is after all a predominantly railway orientated model scene.

Rarely do we see an attempt to place the model truck in its own natural environment or location by attention to surrounding details. Truck modellers could well take a lead from the field of military modelling, where much work has been done in creating small self-contained scenes or dioramas. In these locations a complete area is modelled as a whole – terrain, buildings, vehicles, people – even down to such accessories as maps and mugs of tea. Attempts at creating atmosphere include shell-bursts and pools of water and even lifelike representations of actual personalities instead of anonymous characters. Obviously some detail is obtainable only in the larger scales but it does transform a good model into an excellent one. Often it is this attention to detail which plays a major part in achieving the right atmosphere. Take for instance our common everyday truck. Very rarely is it seen in all its pristine glory as at an indoor exhibition where it is polished and cosseted like a prize cat at a show, with painted tyres and the wheels revolved so that all the tyre names are the same way up.

The real world of the truck is a working one such as a dusty road, a busy transit shed, a muddy quarry or a cobbled street beside a grimy warehouse. Often the vehicle is parked either jacknifed or the steering locked over. Invariably it is part loaded, with the driver humping something or a fork truck fussing over getting a pallet on straight. Perhaps the sheet is folded up on the cab roof and a coiled rope is hung on the door handle. Often the TIR tilt is folded back and the roof sticks and sides removed for better accessibility. But above all it is at least a bit dusty, perhaps even filthy! The truck doesn't stand out of the scene, it nestles into its surroundings because it belongs there.

In real life even the best-kept truck starts to show signs of wear after a while. The fresh paint soon dulls, the tractor is washed more often than the trailer, body sides get damaged by fork trucks, the tyres are muddy, the windscreen gathers a couple of stickers, the tilt cover suffers a little tear and there is scuffing round the manway on a tanker. Whatever the model, a little dirt sprayed judiciously in the right places will add just that touch of much needed realism.

INDEX

Figures in italic refer to illustrations

CREDITS

Jacket front: With substantial 'roo bar', this smart Autocar conventional is typical of the many American trucks used in Australia.

Jacket back: The home-produced Berna is still popular with Swiss truck operators.

Page 1: One of the first 450 hp Caterpillar diesels in Canada was installed in this Kenworth/East dump combination operated by Jules Savard.

Pages 2/3: Hino KB tipper at work in Peru.

Pages 4/5: Volvo drawbar outfit crossing a new bridge built in northern Norway to eliminate ferry delays.